The Embodied Social Justice Workbook

The Embodied Social Justice Workbook explores mindfulness-based practices within a social justice framework, and offers comprehensive guidance to help individuals in marginalized communities deepen their awareness and integrate social justice into their daily lives safely and supportively.

This workbook addresses the critical intersection of mental health, social justice, and mindfulness-based practices, offering valuable insights and tools for practitioners working in these areas. Tailored for individuals and communities navigating marginalization, systemic privilege, and oppression, this book provides a space for readers to engage in mindful practices, document their experiences, and incorporate embodied mindfulness into their daily lives. Chapters explore essential themes such as power and privilege, collective action, creating safe spaces for practice, as well as body mapping and interpreting embodied signals. This hands-on guide is filled with practical exercises and reflection questions as well as lived-experience vignettes to help readers translate practices into their daily lives. It can be used as a companion to *Embodied Social Justice Counseling for Indian Communities* or as a standalone resource.

This book is intended for mental health professionals of all kinds who have an interest in social justice, mindfulness, and especially those who work with clients in the Indian diaspora. It is also a valuable resource for individuals who are interested in engaging in mindful practices and enhancing their awareness of social justice.

Aarathi Selvan, PhD, is a clinical psychologist, founder of Pause for Perspective, and educator integrating mindfulness and embodied social justice into counseling psychology through community practice, teaching, and research in India.

Shoba Nayar, PhD, is a mental health practitioner, qualitative researcher, and educator navigating issues of social justice experienced by marginalized communities in the Indian context.

The Embodied Social Justice Workbook

Exercises for Deepening Practices through Mindfulness

Aarathi Selvan and Shoba Nayar

Routledge
Taylor & Francis Group
NEW YORK AND LONDON

Designed cover image: Getty Image © Benjavis

First published 2027
by Routledge
605 Third Avenue, New York, NY 10158

and by Routledge
4 Park Square, Milton Park, Abingdon, Oxon OX14 4RN

Routledge is an imprint of the Taylor & Francis Group, an informa business

ISBN: 978-1-041-13926-3 (hbk)
ISBN: 978-1-041-13804-4 (pbk)
ISBN: 978-1-003-67220-3 (ebk)

DOI: 10.4324/9781003672203

Typeset in Sabon
by SPi Technologies India Pvt Ltd (Straive)

Access the Support Material: www.routledge.com/9781041139263

Contents

Figures

Preface

Globally, we are living through profound upheaval and transition across political, economic, ecological, and health systems. At the same time, ongoing and intensifying discrimination toward already marginalized communities, including Caste marginalized people, LGBTQ+ people, Indigenous peoples, refugees, and people with disabilities, continues to shape whose lives are made more precarious, whose bodies carry greater risk, and whose suffering is rendered invisible. These realities point urgently toward the need for systemic change. They also raise difficult questions about how injustice is lived, negotiated, and responded to in everyday bodily experience, often long before it becomes visible as advocacy, resistance, or collective action.

It was from this position that, in 2025, we wrote *Embodied Social Justice Counseling for Indian Communities: Integrating Theory and Practice*. As we worked on that text, it became increasingly clear that many of the practices and reflections we were offering, particularly those attending to how social justice is enacted in the body, resonated beyond both the therapeutic context and the Indian setting. We found ourselves wanting to create a space where people could slow down, meet themselves gently, and notice how systems of power, privilege, and oppression are already shaping their embodied responses. This current workbook emerged from that desire.

A Journey into Embodied Social Justice: Deepening Practices Through Mindfulness is not a manual for becoming just, nor a guarantee of transformation. It is an individual-facing offering, created with full awareness of its limits. The practices here invite attention to sensation, impulse, emotion, and response, not because awareness alone produces justice, but because bodies are often responding to injustice long before language, intention, or choice are available.

We recognize that readers do not meet these practices on equal ground. Capacity, safety, risk, and consequence are unevenly distributed. For some, pausing and noticing may feel accessible. For others, it may feel unsafe, exhausting, or irrelevant. Silence, refusal, irritation, and disengagement are not signs of failure in this work. They are meaningful responses shaped by real conditions.

While social justice is often understood at a collective level, through advocacy, policy, redistribution, and resistance, this workbook does not claim that individual reflection can substitute for collective action or structural change. Instead, it offers one site of engagement: a way of noticing how injustice and privilege are lived in the body, how responses emerge under constraint, and how responsibility may become clearer without being simplified.

The practices offered here are situational and provisional. Some may be useful for a time and then fall away. Some may never fit. You are not asked to be consistent, disciplined, or complete. You are invited to stay honest about what is possible under the conditions you are living within.

Aarathi: I am an upper-caste, non-binary, queer and neurodivergent clinician and researcher and the founder of Pause for Perspective. I am also a parent to two wonderful humans and a whole lot of my life is shaped by love for them. My work sits at the intersection of counseling psychology, mindfulness-based practices, narrative approaches, and social justice. Much of what informs this workbook comes from years of clinical practice, teaching, supervision, and community work in India, as well as from my research on how bodies respond to systemic oppression and privilege. I write from within these locations, with ongoing awareness of how power, caste, gender, and access shape both care and responsibility.

Shoba: I am a cis-het, mental health clinician and researcher. My soul story begins in Pondicherry, India where my parents met and married. My physical story commences with my birth in England, where my parents immigrated for my father's work. My family then migrated to Aotearoa New Zealand in the early 1980s, and I was blessed to grow up in that beautiful country. In 2013, however, something stirred inside of me, my body was urging a change; and so, in 2014, I finally listened and immigrated to India. Returning to live in the home of my ancestors has been a powerful journey as I have stumbled my way through learning about how social injustice, oppression, and privilege get enacted in everyday interactions and situations, and the profound implications for people's health and well-being, my own included. As part of this journey, I have had the privilege of working with Aarathi and their team at Pause for Perspective. Through this community I have had the opportunity to experience many of the practices shared in this workbook and witness the work of embodied social justice.

Together, we are excited to welcome you to this workbook and your own journey of deepening into embodied social justice. To that end, we offer this workbook in the spirit of relationship rather than instruction. You may move through it slowly or unevenly. You may skip sections, adapt practices, or set it aside altogether. Nothing here requires completion. For those who are seeking collective spaces to continue reflecting, practicing, or questioning alongside others, we invite you to explore Pause for Perspective's mindfulness sangha, a regular, open space for shared practice and dialogue across contexts and geographies. For more details visit Pause for Perspective's Instagram handle @pauseforperspective

Finally, if this workbook is useful, it will not be because it provides answers. Rather, it will because it helps make visible what bodies already know about care, constraint, and responsibility… and because that noticing does not end at the page.

Author Note

All case vignettes presented in text are composites of clinical experiences and identifying details have been changed to protect the people being discussed and the work itself.

Part I

Setting the Scene

Chapter 1

Introduction to A Journey into Embodied Social Justice

Welcome to your *Journey into Embodied Social Justice: Deepening Practices Through Mindfulness*. A journey is an act of travel, over time, from one place to another. It is not necessarily linear; indeed, sometimes even with the best of planning the intended route can change mid-journey. A journey can be enjoyed as a solo traveler or in the company of others; you may start off with a fully packed bag, only to drop some items along the way and pick up new ones, or perhaps you're the type of person who likes to start with an empty bag, carrying just what you "know," trusting that the rest of the bag will get filled along the way. Whether you embark on this journey as a counselor, someone working within social justice, or simply someone curious about the meeting place of sensation, story, and the world, this workbook is for you. It is not meant as instruction but as companionship on your travels, where your pace and your access needs guide how you move through it.

This is a work shaped by many lineages: mindfulness as developed by Monteiro and Musten;[1] politicized somatics as developed by Staci Haines;[2] polyvagal-informed understandings as taught by Deb Dana;[3,4] narrative practices by Michael White;[5] queer and Mad studies such as the work of Ranade, Chakravarty, Nair, and Shringarpure[6] in queer-affirmative counselling; and the Mad Studies/psychosocial disability perspectives articulated by B. V. Davar.[7] It is further informed by the neurodiversity movement as articulated by Autistic activists of the 1990s and Walker;[8] liberatory psychology as developed by Ignacio Martín-Baró[9] and Maritza Montero[10] and guided by the critical pedagogy of Paulo Freire;[11] and Anti-Caste thought as put forth by many activists and leaders of their respective movements like B. R. Ambedkar,[12] Thenmozhi Soundararajan,[13] Jogdand,[14] Jadhav,[15] and Sophan and Nair.[16]

Last, but by no means least, the text is shaped by disability justice as advanced in the Indian context by Nidhi Goyal and the team at Rising Flame[17] and the collective Blue Dawn,[18] and internationally by Patty Berne and Stacey Milbern of Sins Invalid,[19,20] Mia Mingus,[21] Alice Wong,[22] Leah Lakshmi Piepzna-Samarasinha,[23] and Talila Lewis.[24] Disability justice, in particular, reminds us that the bodymind is not neutral. Some of us sense in ways that are sharp, muted, cyclical, unpredictable, slow, or overwhelming. Some of us sense clearly while moving, stimming, rocking, or holding objects. These variations are not barriers to embodiment; they are part of the body's many languages. Embodied social justice honors all these differences as legitimate ways of knowing.

DOI: 10.4324/9781003672203-2

We begin with sensation; not because it is simple, but because it is already happening. Sensation is the body's first language. The buzz before a sneeze. The melting into a chair after standing for a long time. The relief of cool water on a hot day. The flutter when a meaningful message appears. The drop of the shoulders when encountering someone familiar in a seemingly unfamiliar space.

For many disabled, chronically ill, or neurodivergent people, sensation may not come in predictable, localized forms. It may show up through pain, fatigue, numbness, overwhelm, dissociation, or tension. It may move quickly or arrive slowly. It may be clearer in sound, pressure, or temperature than in interoception. None of these experiences disqualify you. They are all valid entry points into embodied awareness.

The difficulty is not that we cannot feel. It is that many of us have been taught to mistrust or override what we feel. Sensations related to sexuality, trauma, desire, fear, anger, pleasure, or grief have long been moralized or pathologized, particularly within casteist, racist, patriarchal, heteronormative, ableist worlds. Many disabled, mad, and neurodivergent people are additionally told that their bodily experiences are unreliable or excessive. Growing up, many of us received messages like "don't react," "stop being dramatic," "you're imagining it," "calm down," "don't be sensitive." The body's signals become coded as weakness, inconvenience, or danger. So, when invited to tune into sensation, we may feel inadequate, confused, or pressured to find a meaningful answer.

Yet the body continues speaking beneath these inherited stories. Sensation communicates physiologically, physically, emotionally, and relationally. But the meaning we assign to sensation is shaped by caste, race, class, gender, religion, ableism, colonial histories, and access. Sensations often mirror the world we inhabit: maybe tightness before navigating oppressive dynamics, spaciousness when held in belonging, heaviness when silenced, warmth when witnessed.

What would it mean to listen differently? To treat the knot in the stomach before a meeting as information rather than failure? To recognize sensory overwhelm not as personal deficiency but as the body signaling capacity and boundary? To understand numbness or shutdown not as blockage but as protection, often shaped by survival? Sensation becomes a doorway to understanding what the body has been adapting to, resisting, or longing for.

Noticing sensation is not about analysis, diagnosis, or uncovering trauma. It is about building a gentle relationship with your signals—however they present. Sensation does not need to be intense or clear. It does not need to hold insight. It simply needs to be met without judgment. It is honest, immediate, and grounding. It is from this beginning point, the witnessing of sensation, that the rest of the workbook grows.

You might begin by arriving in whatever way is possible. You may be seated, standing, lying down, rocking, pacing, or holding something in your hands. Let your eyes rest or move them gently. Let your attention land on one place in your body that calls you, or one sensation in your environment such as texture, sound, or temperature. It may be vivid. It may be faint. It may feel like nothing at all. Noticing "nothing" is noticing something.

You may describe what you sense in words that hold resonance for you: warm, cool, heavy, stretched, soft, numb, shaky, tired, steady or something else. Or you may reach for images: a rope pulling, a stone resting, a wave rolling, a cloud drifting, or something else. Your metaphors are your body's literature. Naming sensation in your own language is a form of authorship and a refusal of erasure.

In any given moment, sensation may shift or stay steady. It may move, soften, sharpen, pulse, or remain quiet. Staying with it for one slow breath can show you its rhythm. If breath interacts with it, notice that. If it does not, that is also honest. Gradually you may sense need. Not psychological diagnosis but the body's simple longings: rest, movement, grounding, warmth, pacing, space, connection, or quiet. For disabled or neurodivergent bodies, these needs may be influenced by pain cycles, sensory load, fatigue, or shifting capacity or something else. Listening to these needs is solidarity with yourself.

Patterns may become visible over time. Sensations may appear before difficult conversations, when anticipating harm, when feeling held, or when possibility opens. You may observe how posture changes or how environment shapes sensation. Tone of a room, sensory load, accessibility, caste- or race-coded expectations, and power dynamics all influence the body. These are not puzzles to solve. They are stories the body carries. Disabled and marginalized bodies often hold these stories with precision and tenderness.

This is the heart of embodied social justice. You return to the body not to correct it but to listen. You return to sensation not to pathologize but to understand. You return to your bodymind with justice-centered presence. It is with this understanding that we have written, and offer, this workbook.

Stepping into Sensations

As you move through this workbook, do not be surprised if you find that sensation arrives in many different ways. For some people, sitting still brings clarity. For others, sensation becomes easier to meet while moving, rocking, pacing, or stimming. There is no one stillness that the body must achieve in order to be listened to. Movement can be its own form of attention. For many disabled and neurodivergent bodyminds, movement is not simply accommodation; it is intelligence. Rocking, tapping, fidgeting, swaying, changing pressure, or adjusting posture can deepen clarity rather than distract from it. These are forms of knowing, not deviations. Your body senses while swaying, while walking slowly through a room, while adjusting your position, or while holding on to something that grounds you, and in many other ways.

You may notice that some sensations are easier to access through the world outside your skin than the world inside it. For queer and trans people, external sensing may feel safer than internal noticing, especially in environments where the body is scrutinized or misread. The world outside your skin can offer grounding when the world inside carries vigilance or uncertainty. Texture, weight, temperature, and sound can be gentler ways into awareness than internal sensing. Some bodies understand themselves more clearly through the contact of feet on the ground, the feeling of fabric on skin, the coolness of air on the face, or the soundscape in the room. These are not detours from the practice. They are valid doorways into it.

If internal sensing (interoception) feels muted or distant, you might begin with something tangible. Pressure beneath your hands. A surface beneath you. The weight of an object you are holding. A familiar sound. These are not substitutes for sensation; they are sensations. The body speaks in more than one register.

There may be moments when the world feels too loud, too bright, or too much. You are allowed to adjust the environment so that your body can stay present on its own terms.

Earphones, sunglasses, a fidget object, or a weighted item may offer anchoring. Access can also be collective. You might practice stepping into awareness of sensation with someone who helps adjust the environment, offers co-regulation, or supports your sensory needs. Interdependence is a valid and powerful part of embodiment. You might dim the lights, soften the sound, or shift your posture so you can sense without strain. There is no moral value in meeting sensation under difficulty. The practice honors what feels possible to meet with curiosity, not endurance.

Some bodies also move through the world with more ease, greater awareness of sensation, because structures protect them. Dominant-caste, -race, or -class, cis, straight, and non-disabled bodies may notice that stillness, spaciousness, or inward attention comes more readily in certain environments. This is not personal virtue or emotional maturity; it is access that is shaped by safety, by being unmarked, and by being read as "neutral." Noticing this experience, without shame or defensiveness, helps us understand how privilege is carried in the body, and how ease itself can be a form of advantage.

Some of us also navigate environments shaped by caste and class where the body cannot safely soften or close its eyes as a step toward meeting sensation. You may notice your body staying alert or upright in certain rooms. This is not resistance to the practice. It is wisdom shaped by history and survival.

At times, sensation may feel overwhelming or unclear. This is not a sign that you are doing anything wrong. Overwhelm is also the body speaking. If you need to pause, do so; you might look around the room, name a few colors, or simply let your gaze rest on something steady. If you need to step back, slow down, or stop entirely, that is part of the practice. Capacity is not a hindrance; it is guidance. If part of your capacity is shaped by navigating misgendering, gaze, or pressure to perform a certain gendered posture, this too is wisdom. Your body is responding to real conditions. Let that be part of the truth you bring to this practice.

Your sensations may not always be coherent. You may feel too much, too little, or nothing at all. Sensation may arrive as fatigue, pain, numbness, dissociation, sharpness, or distraction. These experiences are not blocks. They are sensations with their own histories and protections. You are not required to make sense of them if they don't naturally arrive. You are only invited to meet them with as much gentleness as the moment allows.

And you are never required to sit still. Embodiment does not ask the body to be quiet, regulated, or calm in order to count. The practice can move with you, follow your rhythms, and adapt to fluctuations in energy, pain, attention, or capacity.

In every part of this workbook, the invitation is the same: let the practice shape itself around you. The work does not ask your body to conform. Let the workbook work for you. Below is a gentle invitation to meet one sensation. Allow yourself to be self-responsive as you approach the practice.

A Short Practice: Meeting One Sensation

Take a moment to arrive in whatever way feels possible right now.

You might be seated, standing, lying down, pacing, rocking, or holding something in your hands.

However your body is situated, is enough.

Some of us may not feel free to soften, settle, or close our eyes in every environment.
If your body stays alert, upright, or watchful, that is not resistance to the practice.
It is wisdom shaped by the histories and worlds you move through—including caste, class, gender, and safety.

And some bodies move with more ease because structures protect them.
Dominant-caste, privileged-race, privileged-class, cis, straight, and non-disabled bodies may find it easier to turn inward.
This ease is not personal virtue. It is access shaped by safety.
Wherever your body is on this spectrum, know that it is welcome here.

When you feel ready, choose a place to sense from that feels most accessible.
This could be something inside your body, something on the surface of your body, or something in contact with the world around you.
Let your body guide you.

Notice one sensation that meets you through this doorway.
For some, it may be warmth, coolness, heaviness, tightness, or stillness.
For others, sensation may arrive as sharpness, fatigue, numbness, tension, shutdown, overwhelm, or "nothing."
All of these are sensations.
None of them are wrong.

Your body is speaking in the language it knows.
Stay with whatever you found.
If words help, name it in your own way:
Warm. Cool. Heavy. Soft. Tight. Still. Buzzing.

Your words are the right words.

Or your own image may meet you:
A wave. A stone. A rope. A cloud.

You might also sense through movement.
A shift in pressure, rocking, fidgeting, tapping, or adjusting your posture can be a form of clarity.
For many disabled and neurodivergent bodyminds, movement is not a distraction—it is intelligence.

Stay with this sensation for one slow breath in and one slow breath out.
Not to change it.
Only to meet it.

If turning inward feels complicated—because of gendered expectations, misreading, surveillance, or the sense of being watched—that too is truth.
Queer and trans bodies often stay partially oriented to the room for safety.
Let your body decide how much inwardness is safe right now.

If the sensation shifts, note that.
If it does not shift, note that too.

When you feel ready, you might ask gently: What might this sensation be asking for right now?
Maybe space.
Maybe rest.
Maybe grounding.
Maybe movement.
Maybe protection.
Maybe dignity.
Maybe simply to be witnessed.
Whatever comes forward is welcome.

Whenever you wish to end, let your awareness return to the room in a way that feels possible for you.
You might notice a sound, a color, a point of contact, or your position in space.

This practice is enough for today.
Your body has already done the work of showing up.

For some of us, showing up means navigating caste or race-coded rooms, sensory load, pain cycles, or gendered vigilance. For others, it may feel easier because the world meets their body with more safety. Naming these differences is also part of embodiment.

Wherever you are, your experience belongs here.

Take a moment to capture your experience—you might use words, symbols, images—whatever feels right for you…

Organization of the Workbook

In *Embodied Social Justice Counseling for Indian Communities*, we presented a range of embodied practices drawing on mindfulness-based processes that Aarathi has adapted and developed as part of Mindfulness Based Symptom Management program that they offer in India. These practices were offered primarily for mental health practitioners to explore by themself, with another person, or with a group. We also shared stories of how people weaved the practices into their lives. In this workbook, you will find scripts for each of those practices that allow you to have a go at using them at a time and space that feels possible for you.

You do not need to be in counseling or have experience in using mindfulness practices to engage with this workbook. You may be actively involved in social justice; or perhaps this is a new space, one you are curious about. If the latter seems more like you, the scripts are intended to provide a scaffold, a framework to start you on your journey of embodied social justice. If you are more experienced with embodied social justice and mindfulness, you may want to adapt the practices themselves. You might rewrite or scribble on the page, circle or underline what feels relevant, change the pacing, shorten a step, or pause midway if your body signals the need. You can shift the practice into drawing, voice notes, movement, or silence. These adaptations are expressions of consent and agency, not deviation. There is no right or wrong way to use this workbook. It is your journey; you chart the path.

To support the practice scripts, we offer mini, lived experience vignettes that feature people experiencing an injustice and how they used the practice to support their journey. In these stories you may perhaps see an aspect of yourself. If that is the case, our hope is that these stories will help you to see how the offered practice may show itself to you and assist on your own journey into embodied social justice. Following the practices, we have crafted reflective questions to further deepen your awareness of the process. Listen to your body for guidance on how to approach these questions—perhaps you feel called to journal your responses, either in words or images; or maybe you want to talk through these questions with another person. Nothing in this workbook is compulsory! How you move through the workbook, what you choose to pack in your bag or leave behind, is your choice and entirely dependent on what feels safe for your bodymind in the moment.

You may notice that certain ideas and invitations are repeated across this workbook; for example, the emphasis on choice, moving at a pace shaped by your body, and letting the practices adapt around you rather than meeting external expectations. This repetition is intentional and rooted in care. Many of us have learned, often through harm, that our bodies must push through, perform understanding, or comply even when something does not feel safe or possible. Repeating these invitations is one way we interrupt that conditioning. This workbook is designed to be entered and exited, returned to, paused, and re-approached over time. You may move back and forth between chapters or practices rather than reading in a linear way. Because of this, we repeat what matters for safety, consent, and access so that wherever you open the book, your body is met with permission rather than demand. If something feels too much, unclear, or inaccessible, that information belongs. Slowing down, skipping, or stopping is not a failure of engagement; it is part of practicing embodied social justice with integrity.

The workbook is divided into four broad parts. The first part is made up of Chapters 1–3. In this first chapter, we have introduced "sensation" as the foundation block upon which this workbook is developed. The next chapter turns to the topic of safety – physical, emotional, cultural. Safety is essential for inviting the body and psyche into social justice work. Chapter 2 offers guidelines for setting personal boundaries, establishing group agreements, and respecting one another's capacities, emphasizing that mindful social justice thrives on kindness, choice, and gentle pacing. Chapter 3 extends out one more layer, connecting personal sensations to broader systemic dynamics, and exploring how these social systems—ability, caste, race, gender, and more—manifest in the body. Through body-scan and breath practices you are invited to take a first step toward reimagining self and society. Journaling prompts help clarify why justice work must include bodily awareness.

Parts II, III, and IV draw from the embodied social justice framework developed by Aarathi in her doctoral research. Part II, Chapters 4 and 5, focus on practices for "Body as a Site of Liberation"; Part III, Chapters 6 and 7, orient towards practices for "Body as a Site of Resistance"; and Part IV, Chapters 8 and 9, turn attention towards practices for "Body as a Site of Resistance." Each of these parts will begin with a recap of the particular focus—Body as a Site of Protest, Resistance, or Liberation—and then offer a range of practices followed by prompt questions to encourage reflection on the practice experience. (If you wish to read more about Body as a Site of Protest, Resistance, or Liberation, you may want to get a copy of the text, *Embodied Social Justice Counseling for Indian Communities*.) We conclude the workbook with Chapter 10, which offers some final ideas for continuing to integrate the practices shared here in your life.

Throughout the workbook, you will find spaces where you can write and journal your reflections. These are not the only spaces. Write, draw, underline, highlight, dog-ear, any of the pages and words that call to you. So, before we start, gather your color pencils, pens, highlighters, maybe even some stickers, whatever brings joy to your body! Sometimes the spaces in workbooks are not enough, or maybe you don't like to mark books; in that case you may also want to get your own journal to accompany this workbook and capture your sensations, feelings, thoughts as you repeat practices over time. At the back of this book, you will also find some pages on Recommended Resources which link to books, poems, Instagram accounts, and other mindfulness or body-associated resources. You may like to add to this list as you discover resources that support your practice.

Before we move into Chapter 2, we offer the following practice as a moment of pause, grounding, orienting to where you hope your journey will take you, and how this workbook might be of support. Before beginning the practice, it is important to remember that meeting the body with safety is not equally available to everyone. Some bodies move through the world with more protection because of caste, race, class, gender conformity, sexuality, skin color, ability, language, or the ways their presence is read as "normal" or "acceptable." These bodies are offered more room to turn inward: fewer threats, fewer interruptions, fewer demands to monitor themselves. Others carry histories of being watched, corrected, misread, or harmed—in families, institutions, medical systems, classrooms, and public spaces—making inward attention more complex. Safety is also shaped by access to stable housing, food, rest, sensory environments, health, community acceptance, and being believed. None of this is personal. It is structural. Naming these differences helps us understand why some bodies find it easier to pause, soften, or sense inwardly, and why for others, arriving with vigilance, numbness, bracing, or hesitancy is a form of truth. Your experience, wherever it lands, belongs here.

Practice Invitation: Arriving into Intention and Gentle Wanting

The hope of this practice is to support in noticing what is present, and gently explore direction or wanting without pressure. You are not seeking clarity or answers. You are simply making room for whatever truth, longing, resistance, or uncertainty lives in you today.

Remember no question is mandatory and if answers don't come it may say something of the way the questions are shaped and how your body is responding to that, and maybe something more. With that in mind, any response is welcome, including "nothing," "I don't know," or silence.

As you begin, you may orient yourself by thinking about different areas of your life: your body, relationships, work, rest, identity, community, today's emotional landscape or something else. You do not need to think about ALL of them. Choose what feels accessible.

Let yourself sense where you are, physically and internally. You may ask:

Where am I as I begin?

____
____
____
____
____
____

What am I carrying right now?

____
____
____
____
____

What do I have capacity for today?

____
____
____
____
____

There is no right way to arrive. If your body feels alert, flat, tense, numb, hopeful, or tired, each of these is valid. Bodies shaped by caste, race, class, gender, disability, queerness, neurodivergence, trauma, or chronic survival may need more time or may not soften at all.

This is not an obstacle; it is wisdom.

You might sense:

Place(s) of tightness in my body

Place(s) where there is more space

Nature of breath (shifts, long, shallow, uncertain…)

You do not need to interpret anything. If sensation feels overwhelming or unreachable orienting to your surroundings is equally valid. Look around the room.

Notice color, temperature, texture of things you can touch and see.

Feel what is under your feet or hands.
Before we move towards wanting, we begin with possibility.

You may ask:

What would make this moment feel a little more possible?

What might help me stay with myself right now?

This could be something simple, like slowing down your pace or adjusting your posture. Or something else. Let whatever comes be enough.

If it feels accessible, you can explore a small inward turn. You may ask:

What do I need from this moment?

How would I like to meet myself right now?

These questions are not about changing anything.

See if you want to bring to the foreground an area of your life you would like to pay attention to for the remainder of this practice (work/career, leisure, relationships [with oneself also], etc.). From here, we gently shift from sensing what is present to exploring what direction or wanting might be possible in an area of life you are holding.

Wanting is shaped by safety and history. For many queer, trans, Dalit, Bahujan, Adivasi, disabled, neurodivergent, or chronically harmed bodies, wanting may feel unfamiliar or risky.

This practice takes that truth seriously.

If wanting feels distant, we begin with:

What feels even a little supportive right now for this area of my life?

Do I have energy for going further with this practice with this area of my life? Do I want to foreground another area or pause here?

(Pause practice here if that feels comfortable and come back to this practice or sift through others that resonate instead)

And if a sense of direction still feels unclear or unsafe within this area of your life, but you would like to explore, turning towards what you do not want can often show you the edges of your capacity and point you gently towards what matters. A protective wanting can also offer direction. Remember you don't have to answer any/all questions if they don't support your answering.

What do I not want in the area I'm exploring through this practice?

What feels like too much for me to hold in this area of my life, given what I am carrying these days?

A "not this" is also wanting. Let your answers be partial, shifting, or uncertain.

Sometimes wanting becomes clearer through noticing what feels true, what part of you is asking for acknowledgment, and what support that part might need. If something inside of you becomes clearer—even gently—you may explore one of these invitations.

Each question builds on the previous one.
First, *locate what is alive in you* (you may choose to write or draw):

What feels true in me today about this area of my life? (This could be an emotion, a sensation, or a quiet recognition or something else.)

Then, sense which part of that truth wants witnessing:
What part of me wants a little more acknowledgment? (This might be a tired part, a hopeful part, a cautious part, a part impacted by today's caste, race, gendered, or disability-shaped interactions or something else.)

Finally, sense what support or presence would help that part move even slightly.
What support might this part need to soften, settle, or simply exist as it is? (Support does not mean solutions. It may look like slowing down, asking for room, taking a pause, adjusting sensory input, or naming a boundary or something else.)

These questions create the bridge towards a declaration without pressure to form one.

If it feels accessible, you may also sense whether a small direction or desire is beginning to form from what you've just named. This is not a question you need to answer clearly; it is simply an invitation to notice if something wants a little space. You might ask:

Is there a small direction I am leaning toward in this area of my life?

____
____
____
____
____

Is there something tiny I am curious about wanting, even if I'm unsure?

____
____
____
____
____

Is there a faint desire whispering inside this part of me?

____
____
____
____
____

These are gentle doorways, not demands. Even the absence of wanting is information.

Before ending, notice how your body is meeting you now.
You do not need to feel settled or clear.
You may feel tender, unsure, grounded, braced, or simply aware or something else.

Choose what helps you transition:
jotting down a word or phrase
resting
drinking water
stepping outside
returning to your day without doing more
or something else

This practice does not require insight.
Arriving is already enough.

You can return whenever something inside you shifts or when you want to listen again.

This practice is shaped from the What do I want? and Declaration practices in the book *Embodied Social Justice in Counseling for Indian Communities: Integrating Theory and Practice*. In exploring what feels true, what asks for acknowledgment, what sets a boundary, what softens, what resists, what reaches, and what refuses, the hope is that you engage with expressions of what you care about for yourself, and for the collective, informed by the body.

By staying close to your body in these gentle ways, you are already in relationship with what matters. The rest of this workbook will continue to support you in accessing the wisdom of your body, at a pace that honors your history, your identities, and your capacity.

References

1. Monteiro LM, Musten RF. Eds. *Practitioner's guide to ethics and mindfulness-based interventions*. Springer. 2017.
2. Haines SK. *The politics of trauma: Somatics, healing, and social justice*. North Atlantic Books. 2019.
3. Dana D. *The polyvagal theory in therapy: Engaging the rhythm of regulation*. WW Norton. 2018.
4. Dana D. *Polyvagal exercises for safety and connection*. WW Norton. 2020.
5. White M. *Maps of narrative practice*. WW Norton. 2007.
6. Ranade K, Chakravarty S, Nair P, Shringarpure G. *Queer affirmative counselling practice: A resource book for mental health practitioners in India*. Mariwala Health Initiative. 2022.
7. Davar BV, Ravindran TKS. Eds. *Gendering mental health: Knowledges, identities, and institutions*. Oxford University Press. 2024.
8. Walker N. *Neuroqueer heresies: Notes on the neurodiversity paradigm, autistic empowerment, and postnormal possibilities*. Autonomous Press. 2021.
9. Martín-Baró I. *Writings for a liberation psychology*. Harvard University Press. 1994.
10. Montero M. *Liberation psychology: Theory, method, and practice*. Springer. 2009.
11. Freire P. *Pedagogy of the oppressed*. Continuum. 1970.
12. Ambedkar BR. *Annihilation of castes: With a reply to Mahatma Gandhi*. Nitin Dhanraj Hanvate Yugashakhi Prakashan. 2023.
13. Soundararajan T. *The trauma of caste: A Dalit feminist meditation on survivorship, healing, and abolition*. North Atlantic Books. 2022.
14. Jogdand YA. Laying the ground for a critical psychology of caste. *J-CASTE* 2024;5(2):49–72. https://www.jstor.org/stable/48778667
15. Jadhav S. Calling the other impure, subhuman is psychological ethnocide. *Outlook India*. 2021. https://www.outlookindia.com/
16. Sophan A, Nair A. Decolonising caste in the Indian context: The psyche of the oppressor. *Psychol Dev Soc* 2023;35(1):110–130. doi:10.1177/09713336231157802
17. Goyal N. Rising flame. *Rising Flame*. https://www.risingflame.org/
18. The Blue Dawn. *The Blue Dawn*. http://thebluedawn.org/
19. Sins Invalid Collective. Skin, tooth, and bone: The basis of movement is our people. *Sins Invalid*. 2019.

20. Berne P. Disability justice: A working draft. *Sins Invalid*. 2015. https://www.sinsinvalid.org/blog/disability-justice-a-working-draft-by-patty-berne
21. Mingus M. Essays on disability justice and access intimacy. 2011–present. https://leavingevidence.wordpress.com/
22. Wong A. Ed. *Disability visibility: First-person stories from the twenty-first century*. Vintage. 2020.
23. Piepzna-Samarasinha LL. *Care work: Dreaming disability justice*. Arsenal Pulp Press. 2018.
24. Lewis T. *Abolitionist disability justice writings*. Various. n.d.

Chapter 2

Creating a Safe Space to Practice

Before we journey deeper into the practices of embodied social justice, it is important to establish how we will engage with the practices and content offered in this workbook. The journey ahead asks you to meet your body's sensations, memories, contexts, and movements with care. It invites you to explore how caste, race, gender, class, disability, neurodivergence, sexuality, language, and other social locations shape the ways your body responds, protects, and seeks connection. Some bodies can turn inward with more ease because the world meets them with more safety. Others find inwardness harder because the internal world holds pain, dysphoria, confusion, overwhelm, or something else making it inaccessible. And for many disabled, neurodivergent, caste- or race-oppressed, queer and trans, and trauma-affected people, the opposite may also be true—inward attention may feel safer than being with the world, because the world is where surveillance, misreading, sensory overload, or threat happens. These differences are structural not personal, and they shape how each of us may enter the practices.

This chapter offers the foundations for a body-centered, safety-focused, and agency-honoring way of practicing. It introduces the conditions—such as choice, pace, access needs, attunement, and collective care—that make it possible to stay with what arises without crossing your limits. It is important to remember that 'choice,' 'pace,' and 'permission' are not equally available to everyone. Dominant-caste or -race, economically resourced, non-disabled, neurotypical, cis, and straight bodies are often, materially speaking, given more room to slow down, feel, or set boundaries without consequence. Marginalized bodies may have had to move quickly, stay vigilant, small, or collapse inward because the world has demanded it. Naming these uneven conditions helps us hold our practices with honesty and dignity. The goal is not to achieve a perfect state of safety but to co-create conditions where your body can participate with as much autonomy, flexibility, and wisdom as possible.

DOI: 10.4324/9781003672203-3

Anaya's Experience of Safety

During a community circle for people with caste marginalization, Anaya began to describe how she often felt invisible in staff meetings at her workplace. As she spoke, her shoulders tightened, her breath grew shallow, and she looked down. A few people around her softened their gaze; one person shifted slightly. The facilitator noticed the room's rhythm and said gently, As I hear you speak, I notice I am bracing by holding my breath, and I notice my jaw has become tight, as if my body is not okay with what happens to you. I wonder what you are noticing about your body, Anaya, and others too.

As the facilitator spoke, a collective exhale moved through the group. Anaya and others shared how their bodies were responding. Her shoulders dropped; her breath grew a little more spacious. Her eyes filled with tears, and she whispered, "I didn't realize my body was holding so much. Hearing others talk about their experience makes me feel very held."

For some people in the room, safety may not have looked like an exhale. It may have shown up as stillness, stimming, rocking, a softening of vigilance, a return of attention, or simply the absence of fear. Safety never has one bodily expression. It does not require openness or relaxation; it includes dissociation that lessens but does not disappear, breath that stays shallow, or vigilance that slowly loosens its grip.

This moment in the circle shows that safety is created not by trying to calm the body but by recognizing what the body is already expressing and allowing that expression to be witnessed. Safety emerges through presence, pacing, clarity, and shared acknowledgment rather than through correction or regulation. The facilitator's openness about their own embodied response invited a relational field of awareness, and the group's willingness to stay with Anaya's experience created a space where no one had to hold their story alone.

This is the kind of relational, body-centered safety that will support you as you move through this workbook. And so, we offer you an invitation to listen to your body without judgment, to notice what arises at your own pace, and to let collective awareness—real and imagined—hold what may feel difficult. Whatever your sensations reveal, whether steady, foggy, tense, numb, shifting, or unclear, your body's way of being here is valid.

This chapter focuses on the conditions that may support creating a safe space to practice the invitations in this book. As you read through these elements, take time to notice what you may need from each one, and how you might make those access accommodations possible for you and the people you practice with.

Cultural and Collective Conditions of Care

Our body's ability to engage with the practices in this workbook is shaped by the world around us. Caste, race, disability, gender identity, class, belonging, and language influence how easily you can settle, how much you protect yourself, and how deeply you can participate. These forces do not wait outside the practice space. They travel with you and shape how your body responds from moment to moment. Further, these intersectionalities are not experienced equally. Some bodies, often those with caste or race privilege, cisnormativity, class security, normative sensory profiles, or dominant language fluency, enter spaces with greater cultural permission to take up room and be understood. Others move through the world with less margin: monitoring tone, managing sensory overwhelm, navigating misgendering, or anticipating caste-, race- or class-based dismissal. These unequal histories shape how easily safety can be accessed or co-created.

Preparing for the journey you will undertake in this workbook includes noticing how these contexts influence your responses. In your everyday life you might find yourself adjusting to meet an unspoken expectation, softening your voice, slowing your movements, or taking up less space. You might feel cautious in some topics or more alert and watchful in others. These responses are meaningful. They reflect the cultural and relational histories your body carries. For many disabled or neurodivergent people, these adjustments may also include managing sensory load, avoiding overstimulation, masking, or using alternative forms of communication. For queer and trans people, these shifts may reflect histories of hypervisibility, erasure, or relational misrecognition. These embodied responses are not overreactions, they are wisdom shaped by experience.

Acknowledging these influences allows you to participate in ways that feel respectful and true to your lived experience. Later chapters may invite you into sensations shaped by these systemic histories. Therefore, recognizing contextual influences will help you respond with compassion instead of judgment. It also prepares you to adapt each practice based on what your body needs, which is essential for safe and honest engagement.

Attending to these cultural and collective conditions of care also invites us to gently notice who or what supports us as we engage in this work. Many of us were taught to turn inward alone, to self-manage, or to not rely on others. Yet bodies are shaped in relationship, and they often find steadiness, meaning, and safety through shared presence. The following practice offers a way to reflect on what community, witness, or shared care might look like for you as you move through this workbook, in ways that honor both your access and your limits.

Mapping Collective Conditions of Care

This is a practice for inviting community into your workbook journey.

This workbook can be done alone, but it was not designed to be held only by one body. Many of us have learned to survive by carrying things privately. This practice gently explores who or what might support you to stay resourced as you move through these pages.

You do not need to already feel safe with others to begin this work. You are only being invited to notice what feels possible.

Take a few moments to settle your body in whatever way helps you feel oriented. You might notice your contact with the floor, your breath, or an object near you.

Now, without pressure to decide anything yet, slowly reflect on the following:

1 Who helps your body feel less alone?

This could be:

- A friend, colleague, partner, therapist, teacher
- A group space, online, or in person
- A community, political collective, faith space, creative space
- Even a pet, a place, a memory, or a routine

You might write one name. You might write a few names. You might write none. All options are okay.

____
____
____
____
____
____

2 How does your body know support is present?

When you think of this person/s, space, or presence, what shifts in your body, if anything?

- Does your breath change?
- Does your vigilance soften?
- Do you feel more alert, steadier, quieter, or more held?
- Or do you feel unsure, conflicted, or guarded?

There is no right response. Noticing is enough.

____
____
____
____
____
____

3 What kind of support feels possible right now?

Support does not have to mean sharing everything. It may look like:

- Sitting quietly together while you do a practice
- Checking in by message after a difficult exercise
- Doing one reflection aloud instead of alone
- Being witnessed without advice

You might complete this sentence gently:
The kind of support that feels most doable for me right now is

4 **What support is *not* available, and how does your body respond to that?**

If you notice grief, anger, numbness, or resignation here, that response also carries meaning.

You are not broken for needing care that was unavailable. Many bodies learned to survive without it.

You might simply name: *One kind of care that feels missing or hard to access for me right now is*

5 **A choice, not a demand**

If it feels right, you may choose one small step toward shared practice. If it does not, you may choose to keep your practice private for now. Both are forms of agency.
You might choose to:

- Tell someone you are working through this book
- Invite someone into one small practice
- Let a trusted person know when you feel overwhelmed
- Consciously choose solitude as your condition of safety for now

In this moment, I choose to:

6 Closing reflection for the exercise

You might place a hand somewhere on your body that conveys care and acknowledgment:
My body's way of finding care makes sense in the context of my life.
Perhaps there is another similar recognition you want to offer in your own words:

There is nothing you must fix here. This is not a checklist of relational success. This is simply a way of recognizing that your nervous system, your history, and your structural location all shape how community feels possible.

Safety as Co-Held

Safety does not arise only from your inner work with your body. It is also shaped by how others witness you, how they listen, and how they hold their own presence beside yours. In community and relational practices, safety is co-created. Your ability to stay with what arises often depends on how the space around you responds when you reveal even a small truth. Safety in relational spaces is not evenly available. Caste, race, class, gender expression, disability, neurodivergence, queerness, and other marginalizations shape who is listened to without suspicion, who is granted emotional room, and whose truth is met with defensiveness. Some bodies move through the world being routinely validated; others have learned that being witnessed can invite risk, misinterpretation, or correction. Co-held safety in this workbook honors these differences so you never have to perform openness, and you never have to reveal more than what feels possible.

Think of a time when someone listened to you without trying to fix anything. Their steady breath, softened eyes, or quiet presence may have helped your body settle. Or you may remember a moment when another person's kindness made it possible for you to stay with something that felt difficult. These experiences show how relational presence supports the body's capacity to engage with honesty and care. Oftentimes these experiences slip by quietly; take a moment here to write down a time you experienced relational presence, what happens in your body as you bring that experience into the present?

I remember a time when…

For many disabled or neurodivergent people, relational presence does not always look like direct eye contact, stillness, or steady breath. Safety may come through stimming, pacing, avoiding gaze, holding an object, typing instead of speaking, or sensing another's presence without needing closeness. Queer and trans bodies may feel safer when witnessing is quiet, non-intrusive, and does not assume familiarity. These alternative forms of co-presence are not deviations, they are legitimate relational languages.

Although you may complete many of the practices in this workbook on your own, you are not practicing in isolation. You carry relationships, communities, and histories with you. You can also choose to practice with someone you trust, form a small reflective group, or check in with an accountability partner who understands this work. These relational possibilities are part of your safety net. Even when you practice alone, co-held safety can still be created. You can imagine someone whose presence feels steady, or you can place an object nearby that reminds you of accompaniment. Take a few minutes to note below the relationships, communities, and histories you carry:

Relationships	**Communities**	**Histories**
☐	☐	☐
☐	☐	☐
☐	☐	☐
☐	☐	☐
☐	☐	☐
☐	☐	☐
☐	☐	☐

It also matters to name that not all bodies enter reflective spaces with the same histories of safety. Some have experienced relational rupture, surveillance, or coercive forms of 'listening.' For caste or race-privileged, cis-passing, able-bodied people, relational spaces may have been protective; for marginalized communities, they may have been sites of harm. This workbook invites you to draw from the relationships that feel sturdy, whether chosen family, comrades, peers, or imagined figures who embody non-hierarchical care. When you approach this workbook with the understanding that safety is co-held, you do not place the burden of safety solely on your individual effort. You recognize the relational threads that support your engagement and the many ways presence, companionship, and permission can accompany you through this work.

Some practices in this workbook may bring up sensations or emotions that feel easier to meet when you imagine or receive steady presence. Understanding safety as something co-held helps you stay connected to yourself without pushing or withdrawing. It prepares you for any exercises that involve partners or community, and it reminds you that connection can be a resource even when practiced at a distance. When you recognize that presence can be offered and received in multiple forms, you expand the possibilities for safety throughout the workbook.

Because safety is co-held, not extracted, this workbook centers consent, pacing, and access needs in relational practices. You decide how close or how distant a practice feels. You choose the modality of expression. And you decide whose imagined, remembered, or present companionship supports your capacity. Safety grows when relationships honor autonomy rather than assume intimacy.

Practice Invitation 1: Mutual Tending

(8 to 10 minutes)

This practice invites you to experience safety as something that forms through presence rather than through fixing, advice, or performance. You may practice with a partner, or you may practice alone with imagined, remembered, or symbolic presence.

For now, we stay with what feels neutral, steady, or gently pleasant. The hope is that it may support your nervous system to build safety before meeting harder material later in the workbook.

Before You Begin

Choose the modality that best supports your bodymind in this moment. You may speak, write, type, draw, move, stim, or remain quiet.

If you are practicing alone, you may imagine that your words or movements are being witnessed by someone whose presence feels steady and non-demanding. This presence could be a friend, teacher, therapist, elder, or colleague who once listened without rushing or fixing. It could be a grandparent, ancestor, chosen family member, or even a character from a book or film who represents steadiness, dignity, or protection. For some, this presence may be a pet who stays close without expectation, a tree, river, room, or familiar place where the body has felt settled, or a simple object such as a stone, shawl, book, or photograph that carries meaning. This presence does not need to speak, guide, or respond in any way. It does not even need to be real, alive, or human. It only needs to feel steady enough for your body to sense accompaniment rather than aloneness.

You may stop early.
You may pause.
You may change how you participate at any point.

Option 1: Verbal or Written Mutual Tending

Step 1: Speaking or Expressing (Positive and Neutral Focus)

If paired: One person speaks for 2 minutes about *one small, neutral, or steady thing that feels present right now*. This does not have to be emotional or meaningful. You may choose from:

- Something in your body that feels okay enough right now
- A moment from today that felt ordinary, steady, or slightly pleasant
- A neutral sensation such as warmth, weight, breath, or contact
- Something simple you are looking forward to in the near future
- What it feels like to sit here in this moment
- Or something else that is neutral or steady that feels present right now

You may move slowly. You may pause often. Simple description is enough.

If alone: Write, speak aloud/actively think, draw, or move with one of the same entry points for 2 minutes.

Step 2: Sensing Presence

If paired: The listener notices their own body while listening. You may track breath, shoulders, jaw, hands, belly, or any subtle shift. There is no need to respond, interpret, or reassure.
If alone: Pause and notice how your body responds to your own words or expression.

Step 3: Simple Reflection

If paired: The listener reflects one brief, body-based observation, such as:

> "As you spoke, I noticed my breath slow" or "My shoulders dropped as I listened."
> No advice. No analysis. Only a simple act of noticing.

If alone: Write or think one similar sentence to yourself.

Step 4: Switching (If Paired)

Switch roles and repeat the steps.

Option 2: Fully Non-Verbal Mutual Tending

(For those who prefer not to speak or write)

If paired: One person becomes the 'present body.' The other becomes the 'witness.' For 2 minutes, the present body:

- Breathes
- Moves gently
- Rocks
- Holds an object
- Or simply sits

There is no performing. Only being.

The witness notices their own body quietly while staying nearby. After 2 minutes, the witness offers **one simple sentence** such as:

- "I noticed my breath slow."
- "My body felt steadier as I sat with you."
- "My shoulders softened."

Switch roles.

If alone: Sit with an object, a wall, a plant, or your own hands for 2 minutes. Notice your body. Then write or think one simple sentence of bodily noticing.

Reflection After Tending

You may reflect through writing, drawing, silence, or movement. Choose one or two questions only. You do not need to answer all.

- Did anything in your body shift even slightly while being witnessed or witnessing? (*breath, shoulders, jaw, stomach, pace, attention*)

- Was there a moment that felt steady, simple, or okay enough? What helped that happen, if anything?
- How did the way the listening happened affect your body? (*the silence, pacing, reflection, absence of fixing*)
- Which kind of presence felt most supportive through this practice? (*choose from: silence, distance, voice, movement, stimming, objects, writing, or simply being alongside*)

Noticing is enough. Insight, though welcome if it comes, is certainly not required.

This practice is not about doing it 'right.' It is about noticing how safety forms through shared presence, even in quiet or minimal ways. You do not need to push for closeness. You do not need to resolve anything. You are only being invited to feel how accompaniment, real or imagined, can soften the work of staying with what is present.

As you continue through the workbook, you may choose one steady presence you can call on when needed, or keep a small object nearby that helps you feel companioned. You do not have to move through these practices alone.

Listening to the Body's Language

Your body communicates through sensation long before words arrive. These sensations might feel like warmth, tightness, heaviness, lightness, fogginess, pressure, tingling, or stillness. Sometimes sensations come gently. Sometimes they arrive all at once. For people who carry trauma or chronic stress, sensations can feel intense or unclear. For many neurodivergent, disabled, queer or trans, and caste- or race-oppressed bodyminds, sensations may also feel muted, mixed, dysphoric, confusing, or shaped by long histories of masking and vigilance. These variations are not barriers to embodiment. They are part of the body's honest ways of speaking.

What sensations does your body use to communicate? Write them down and maybe draw them in the picture below.

You can find a template of this image in Appendix A. You may want to copy it and fill it out at different times as you progress through this workbook and become more aware of how your body is speaking to you (Figure 1).

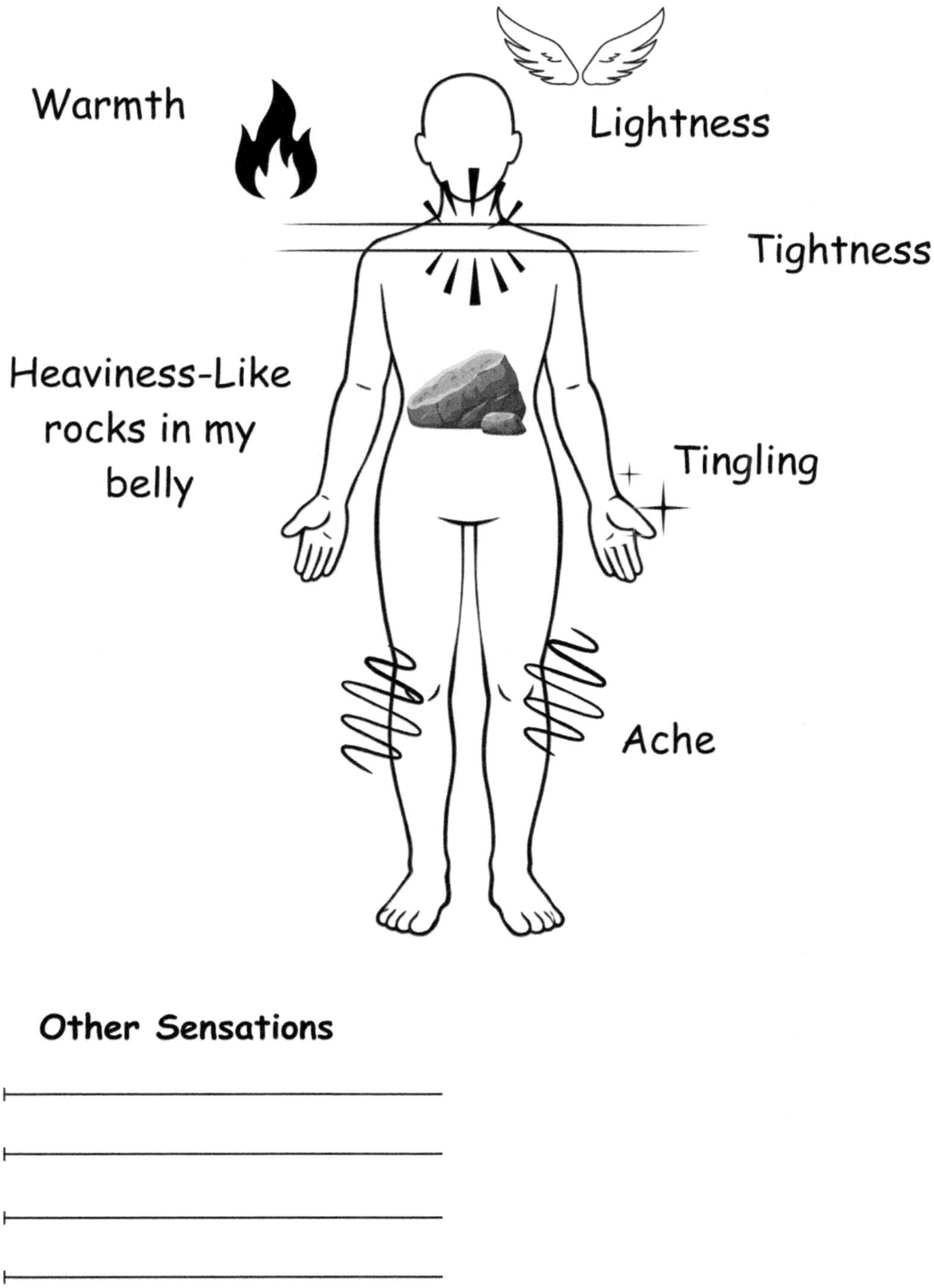

Figure 1 Body Sensations.

Listening to your body does not require you to stay inward. You can sense from the outside as well. Looking around the room, feeling the chair beneath you, noticing sound, or moving gently are also forms of embodied attention. For some people, especially those with sensory sensitivity or past experiences of scrutiny or dysphoria, sensing outward may feel safer than sensing inward. This is not avoidance. It is a valid way the body stays oriented and protected.

Listening is not about going in with an agenda or need to fix oneself. It is about learning how your body communicates and letting that shape your pace and choices. As you begin to notice sensation, you may also become aware of the feeling tone that comes with it, a sense of ease, hesitation, pull, or pause that starts to guide your direction. Some sensations may feel like they are signaling that something is welcome. Some may feel like they are signaling caution. Some may feel mixed, muted, or hard to name. Sometimes there may be numbness, over-alertness, dissociation, or confusion instead of clarity. These are not failures of listening. They are expressions of history, protection, and survival.

Sometimes, listening to the body brings what might seem ordinary and necessary, such as hunger, thirst, exhaustion, pain, or the need for warmth, movement, or rest. These are not separate from emotion or insight. They are often the way emotion and meaning arrive in the body. Realizing you are hungry, overwhelmed, in need of pause, or longing for contact can be the very insight the body is offering. In these moments, responding to what the body asks for is also part of listening. Eating, stretching, pausing, using the bathroom, lying down, drinking water, or stepping outside are not distractions from the practice. They are expressions of care. Listening is not about fixing yourself. It is about allowing what matters to become apparent through the body and tending to it with dignity rather than override.

As safety is shaped through both shared presence and your wider conditions of care, listening to the body becomes possible when it is approached gently, with choice, and without force.

Practice Invitation 2: Sensing from the Outside and the Inside

(8 to 10 minutes, adaptable)

This practice supports listening to your body in a way that stays within safety and choice. You may sense from the outside, from the inside, or move gently between the two. There is no right order and no correct experience.

Choose a posture that feels steady enough for you.
You may sit, stand, lean, or lie down.
You can keep your eyes open or let them soften.
You may pause or stop at any point.

Step 1: Begin with the Outside

Sensing the environment around you

Let your attention rest on one external anchor. This could be:

- A sound in the room
- The feeling of the floor beneath your feet
- The support of the chair or wall
- Something you can see in front of you
- The temperature of the air on your skin
- Or something else that you are able to place your attention on

Name your anchor: ______________________________

Notice what this outside anchor feels like. Steady, neutral, soothing, distracting, or something else. Whatever you notice is simply information. If nothing stands out clearly, that is also okay.

How does this anchor feel?

Step 2: Gently Check Inside

Sensing your body from within

If, and when, you feel ready, notice one place inside your body that feels a little more available than the rest.

Not comfortable. Not open. Just a little more available.

This might be noticed as:

- Your breath as it moves in and out
- The weight of your hands or legs
- Tightness or softness in your jaw or shoulders
- The rise and fall of your chest
- Warmth, heaviness, or pressure somewhere in your body

You may notice this in stillness or through a small movement, such as:

- Shifting your weight
- Rocking gently
- Stretching slightly
- Changing your posture

I noticed…

If nothing inside feels available today, return to the outside. This may be your body protecting you from overwhelm, pain, dysphoria, or sensory overload. That protection also deserves respect.

Step 3: Move Between the Two

Slowly shift your attention:

- From the outside anchor
- To the inside sensation or movement
- And back to the outside again

You might go back and forth a few times.
Move at your own pace. There is no need to stay anywhere for long.

This movement between outside and inside helps your body stay within its capacity and supports listening without becoming overwhelmed. Your capacity is shaped by history, identity, and what your body has survived. It is not a measure of strength.

Step 4: Ask One Gentle Question

Choose one question that feels possible today:

- What is this sensation communicating?
- Does this feel like welcome, caution, or something else?
- What might this sensation be asking for right now, such as rest, movement, nourishment, contact, or something else?
- Let your body respond in its own way. You are not looking for words. A shift, a pause, a tightening, a softening, or even no change at all is still a response.

Use this space to write down your answer to one of the above questions.

Step 5: Come Back to the Outside

Before ending the practice, gently orient again to your surroundings.

- Look around the room
- Name three objects or three colors
- Feel the support beneath you

Let your body know that the practice is ending.

Reflection

You may reflect in writing, silence, drawing, or movement. Choose one question only.

- What felt easier to sense today: the outside or the inside?
- What helped you stay connected, if anything?
- Did any sensation feel familiar?
- What do you notice now about how your body communicates?

Use this space to write down your answer to one of the above questions.

If what you notice is that your body communicates in ways that feel unclear, muted, inconsistent, or shaped by past harm, that knowing is also meaningful. Confusion is a form of communication.

Listening to your body is not about solving anything. It is about learning the rhythm in which your body speaks and giving yourself the dignity of hearing it. If listening inward does not feel accessible today, listening outward to sound, support, movement, or contact is also listening. Your body will choose what makes sense right now.

Choice, Pace, and Permission

A space is only practiceable when people know they have genuine choice. In oppressive systems, bodies often learn that they cannot say no, cannot pause, cannot slow down, and cannot opt out. By explicitly naming choice, we restore dignity. Choice includes:

- the choice to pass
- the choice to take a break
- the choice to change posture or the modality of a practice
- the choice to hold back or to lean in
- the choice to adjust based on access needs

These choices have never been equally available. Caste or race-oppressed, disabled, queer, trans, and neurodivergent bodyminds have often been denied refusal, rest, slowness, and inwardness, while dominant-caste or -race, able-bodied, neurotypical, cis, and economically resourced bodies are more readily granted pause, patience, and accommodation when they choose their pace. These uneven permissions shape how each of us arrives here. For some, choosing a slower pace may feel unfamiliar, risky, or even impossible. For others, it may feel expected.

Pace is not just about speed. Pace is about capacity. It is about how much your body can take in, stay with, and respond to in this moment without having to brace, shut down, fragment, or override itself. This capacity changes from day to day and moment to moment. These shifts are not lack of commitment. They are the body adjusting to what is possible now.

The pace your body carries is not created in isolation. It is shaped by the same structural conditions that shape access to choice. Many marginalized bodies have learned to move quickly, stay alert, mask distress, comply, or remain silent to survive. Over time, this urgency becomes the body's default rhythm. What feels like 'your pace' today is not a personal trait. It is a history written into the body.

For disabled and chronically ill people, choice is also shaped by fluctuating capacity. Pain cycles, fatigue, sensory overload, and shifting executive functioning can determine what is possible on any given day. When your body reaches its limits, this is not avoidance. It is information. Capacity is not a barrier to this practice. It is part of the practice.

Engaging with this workbook means trusting the pace you carry rather than correcting it. Giving your body permission to pause, open your eyes, shift position, move, rest, skip a section, or stop a practice entirely is not resistance. It is consent. It is a way of saying that your body's limits are meaningful.

Letting the body set the pace also means recognizing that staying with something and stepping back from something are both valid movements. Slowing down is not always avoidance. Stopping is not always failure. Speeding up is not always growth. Stillness is not always safety. Your body chooses its pace in response to pain, fatigue, dysphoria, sensory load, emotional saturation, relational context, and what it has learned about permission and danger. There is no single correct rhythm for practice.

Sometimes the body will guide you toward very simple actions: resting, eating, drinking water, stretching, using the bathroom, stepping outside, lying down, or becoming quiet. These are not interruptions to the work. They are the work of maintaining capacity. Responding to these needs is one way the body preserves its ability to remain in relationship with experience rather than pushing past itself.

When choice is acknowledged, the body does not have to brace itself. When pace is respected, the body does not have to perform. When permission is explicit, the body can remain dignified. Without choice, you may push through discomfort because you believe you must. Without pace, you may override your needs.

Letting the body set the pace interrupts inherited rhythms of caste hierarchy, productivity, urgency, and compliance. In this workbook, you are not asked to keep up. You are invited to keep time with your body.

Practice Invitation 3: Letting Your Body Choose the Pace

(6–8 minutes, highly adaptable)

Before You Begin

Remember that you get to decide how you participate. This practice does not ask you to go inward unless your body chooses to. Your only task is to notice the pace at which your body wants to move, or whether it wants to move at all.

For many neurodivergent bodies, interoception may be muted, inconsistent, or overwhelming. Attention may anchor more easily in movement, sound, rhythm, or patterned visual focus rather than internal cues. Choosing 'I do not want to sense anything closely right now' is not a retreat. It is an affirming boundary that honors how your body communicates.

1 *Offer your body three options*

Silently offer yourself three possibilities:

- Option 1: I want to stay with something external.
- Option 2: I can sense something inside for a moment.
- Option 3: I do not want to sense anything closely right now.

Let your body choose.

Wait for the smallest cue: a breath, a shift, a softening, a pull, or nothing at all.

My body chooses Option: ______________________________

If you are queer or trans, you may notice that certain choices like posture, breath, stillness, or gaze feel shaped by how your body has been watched, policed, or misgendered in the world. The way you choose or avoid certain anchors may reflect long histories of safety-seeking. This is not resistance to the practice. It is your intelligence at work.

2 *Follow that choice for just 15–20 seconds*

- If your body chose the outside: stay with a sound, a color, or a texture.
- If your body chose the inside: stay with one small sensation.
- If your body chose neither: stay exactly as you are.

3 *Ask your body if it wants to continue, pause, change, or stop*

Again, wait for the smallest signal.

- If your body wants to continue, stay for another 15 seconds.
- If it wants to pause, shift your gaze or position.
- If it wants to change the anchor, allow it.
- If it wants to stop, end the practice.

Permission builds capacity more than endurance ever could.

4 *End with orientation*

Look around the space.
Let your body know the practice is ending.
Feel the ground beneath you.

Reflection

How did your body tell you which option to choose?

What pace felt possible, and what pace felt too much?

What shifted when you gave yourself permission to stop or change mid-practice?

What does this tell you about how your body wants to move through this workbook?

Pace is relational, not internal alone. It is shaped by caste location, disability, gendered scrutiny, neurodivergence, access, and the environments we have survived. Some bodies can slow down without consequence. Others have had to move quickly, stay vigilant, or remain invisible to survive. Honoring your body's pace is an act of liberation. It is how the work ahead becomes livable.

Recognizing, Not Regulating

In many systems, regulation has meant control. It has meant learning how to contain distress so it does not disrupt others, how to quiet intensity so it appears acceptable, how to override the body so one can continue to function within dominant expectations. For many marginalized bodies, regulation has been demanded as obedience: be calm, be reasonable, be productive, be quiet, be composed. These demands have never been evenly distributed. Caste, class, gender identity, disability, neurodivergence, and queerness shape whose expressions are tolerated and whose are punished, medicalized, or disciplined.

Because of this history, this workbook does not begin with regulation as the goal. It begins with recognition. Recognition means letting the body be seen as it is. Agitation, numbness, tears, tremors, heat, tightness, shutdown, dissociation, restlessness, or clarity are not problems to be corrected. They are communications shaped by the lives we have lived and the worlds we have survived. Some bodies are allowed to express distress without consequence. Others are not. When we begin with recognition, we interrupt the idea that the body must first be fixed in order to be worthy of care.

For disabled and neurodivergent bodyminds, expression may include sensory overwhelm, stimming, masking fatigue, fluctuating attention, pain cycles, or shutdown. These are not failures of the practice. They are how the body speaks under real conditions. For queer and trans bodies, expression may be shaped by histories of scrutiny, dysphoria, misrecognition, or hypervisibility. For caste- or race-oppressed bodies, expression may carry vigilance, silence, or restraint learned through social threat. Recognition means allowing these expressions to exist without forcing them into dominant templates of calm, clarity, or coherence.

At the same time, recognition does not mean doing nothing. When the body is met with honesty and dignity, it often reveals what it needs to remain in relationship with life. Sometimes that need may look like slowing down, stepping back, seeking support, changing an environment, naming a boundary, or asking for accommodation. From the outside, this may resemble 'regulation.' But in embodied social justice, this movement does not arise from control or correction. It arises from listening.

> This is the crucial difference:
> Regulation aimed at control asks, "How do I make this stop?"
> Recognition aimed at liberation asks, "What is this response trying to protect, express, or make possible?"

When recognition leads to action, that action is not about fitting into oppressive systems. It is about staying in relationship with what you care about for yourself and for the collective. It is about preserving capacity, dignity, and connection. This is how recognition becomes the ground for wise response, rather than compliance.

Recognition also includes recognizing when staying with sensation is too much. You are not required to remain with anything that feels overwhelming, unsafe, or destabilizing. Stepping back, looking around the room, shifting your posture, pausing, or stopping entirely are all ways the body preserves its capacity to participate. This is not avoidance. It is intelligence.

In Chapter 1, you explored what you want and what you might be willing to declare, even in small ways. This chapter has been about building the conditions that allow that wanting to be met with care rather than force. Recognition is the bridge between these two. It is how the body says, "This is what is true right now," without immediately being shaped into performance, productivity, or calm.

The practices that follow in the workbook will invite deeper noticing, sitting with, and responding. But for now, we want to remind you that nothing needs to be mastered in advance. Your body does not need to arrive regulated in order to be welcome here. It only needs to be met.

Closing Practice 4: Returning to the Field

(3–4 minutes, optional)

This is not a settling practice. It is a recognition practice.

Before you begin, choose a posture that feels workable. You may sit, stand, lean, lie down, rock, pace, or hold an object. You may keep your eyes open or closed. Let your body choose how it wants to be here.

Gently notice the environment around you.
A sound.
The air on your skin.
The surface beneath you.
Let the room share some of the work of holding you.

Now bring attention to one place in your body that feels available right now.
Not comfortable.
Not calm.
Just available enough to notice.

It may feel quiet, tired, neutral, warm, restless, steady, heavy, unclear, or blank.
Let that be enough.

Without searching, allow your body to offer one small response from this moment.
This may be a word, an image, a gesture, a shift in posture, a breath or nothing at all.
Whatever arises is your body's way of speaking today.

Now gently widen your awareness so that you are sensing your body, and the space around you at the same time.

When you feel ready, you may end in whatever way helps you transition:

- placing a hand somewhere
- changing position
- opening your eyes
- or simply moving on.

Reflection

Choose one only.

- What felt most available in your body just now?
- What did your body offer from this moment, if anything?
- What might this response be communicating about what you need as you close?
- What is one small thing you want to offer yourself as you move into the rest of your day?

Use this space to write down your answer to one of the above questions.

Recognizing your body's responses without forcing calm, control, or resolution creates room for this work to remain alive. Some bodies have been required to regulate for survival. Others have been rewarded for appearing composed. In this workbook, your body does not have to perform either role. Let it speak in its own rhythm, shaped by history, identity, and lived experience. This is how you move forward with dignity, truth, and choice.

Integration: My Conditions of Care

Creating your own map of care is one of the ways you prepare your body to move through the rest of this workbook with steadiness. When you take time to name what helps you stay connected, what signals protection, and what supports your capacity to participate, you are building a foundation that can travel with you through the work ahead.

This is your personal map. A living guide you can return to, revise, and expand as you learn more about what your body needs. While it is personal, it is not created in isolation. The conditions that make steadiness possible are not evenly distributed. Caste, race, class, disability, queerness, neurodivergence, gender identity, and language shape who has access to spaciousness, privacy, sensory comfort, and relational support. Some bodies can set boundaries with ease. Others must remain vigilant because the environments they move through are surveilling, caste-coded, heteronormative, or ableist. Naming this helps you recognize that your needs are shaped by context, not by individual shortcomings.

For neurodivergent or disabled bodyminds, these conditions of care may include sensory supports, pacing that honors fluctuating capacity, predictable structure, alternative communication, rest, or stimming. For queer and trans people, care may include chosen family, identity-affirming presence, or spaces where gender expression is not questioned or scrutinized. These forms of care are not optional. They are essential to participation with dignity.

It is also true that some bodies are granted more room to rest, pause, or feel than others. Privilege often determines whose exhaustion is taken seriously and whose discomfort is ignored, disciplined, or made invisible. As you build your map, you may choose to name not only what supports you, but also what conditions of care have been historically denied or unevenly available to you. This naming is part of reclaiming your body's truth.

Safety is not the absence of difficulty.
It is the presence of care.
It is the willingness to pace, to listen, to pause, and to honor each body's truth.
It is created through context, relationship, and choice.
It grows when we trust that our aliveness, in all its forms, belongs here.

This integration is not meant to be finished. It is a living map you can return to whenever the work feels tender, unclear, or alive in new ways.

You may begin mapping your conditions of care here.

Another version of this map can be found in Appendix B.

When my body begins to protect me, I usually feel:	*This often happens when:*
This reveals something about the environment, relationship, or situation, namely that:	*What helps me return to connection is* – You might include: • a sound or texture that grounds you • a posture that supports you • a person, place, or memory that feels like home • an access aid or sensory support that makes participation more possible

As you continue, you may notice that sensations, reflections, and memories arise not only from your inner world but also from the systems and histories that have shaped your access to care. The foundations you explored in this chapter, listening to your body's responses, practicing at your own pace, honoring choice, recognizing without forcing regulation, and tending to collective conditions of care, are what make it possible to meet the chapters ahead with depth and dignity.

With this grounding in place, we now invite you to move further into your body as a site of social life, meaning, and response.

Chapter 3

Embodied Social Justice

When we use the phrase embodied social justice, we are not referring to justice as an idea, belief system, or set of values held only at a cognitive or ideological level. Nor are we suggesting that bodily awareness, by itself, produces social change. Instead, embodied social justice[1] names a way of noticing how systems of power, oppression, and privilege are already lived and negotiated through the body, often before language, choice, or conscious intention are available.

Bodies respond continuously to social conditions.[2–5] They brace in rooms shaped by caste hierarchy. They tighten in the presence of surveillance or misrecognition. They soften when safety is offered. They shut down, speed up, freeze, comply, refuse, or adapt in ways that reflect real risks and uneven access to protection. Embodied social justice begins by recognizing these responses not as personal shortcomings or psychological traits, but as intelligent adaptations shaped by history, structure, and survival.

In this workbook, embodiment is not treated as a neutral or universal experience. Bodies do not enter the world on equal terms. Ability, caste, race, class, gender, sexuality, neurodivergence, chronic illness, and access shape whose bodies are granted rest, whose pain is believed, whose emotions are tolerated, and whose boundaries are respected. Because of this, embodied social justice does not ask all bodies to sense in the same way, move at the same pace, or arrive at the same conclusions. It asks instead: What is this body responding to, and under what conditions?

Embodied social justice is, therefore, not about regulating the body into calm, insight, or coherence. It is about recognition before response. It involves staying close to sensation, impulse, hesitation, refusal, or discomfort long enough to understand what these responses are protecting, resisting, or making possible. From this place, response may take many forms, including boundary setting, withdrawal, redistribution of effort, repair, collective action, or choosing not to act at all.

This chapter invites you to begin noticing how social systems show up somatically in your own life. Not so you can fix yourself, perform awareness, or extract clarity, but so you can build a more honest relationship with how your body has learned to live under the conditions you inhabit. What follows is not a diagnostic exercise. It is an invitation to witness how justice, injustice, and responsibility are already being carried, moment by moment, in the body.

DOI: 10.4324/9781003672203-4

In the first two chapters, you were invited to listen to sensation, to approach the body through recognition rather than correction, and to move at a pace shaped by capacity and conditions of care. This chapter builds on that foundation by turning more directly toward how systems such as caste, race, gender, disability, sexuality, class, and neurotypical norms live in the body as posture, breath, vigilance, collapse, ease, or bracing.

We do not carry social systems only in our thoughts. We carry them in how we tighten, hesitate, expand, prepare for impact, and learn when it is safe or unsafe to be visible. These bodily patterns are not personal flaws; they are histories held in the body. They also do not remain private. How bodies brace, withdraw, collapse, or stay alert shapes how classrooms are held, how meetings unfold, how therapy and supervision are structured, how safety is imagined, and how leadership is embodied. Noticing the body in this way is not only about personal insight. It can inform how we question institutional norms around pace, silence, productivity, authority, and who is expected to adapt.

Mira: When Shaping Becomes Visible in Ordinary Moments

In a meeting at work, a casual remark is made about caste-reservation in universities "lowering standards." It is said lightly, almost as a joke. Many people in the room do not register it. Mira does. Before she has time to think, her stomach tightens. Her breath becomes shallow. Her shoulders pull inward. She says nothing. Speaking up would carry real consequences for her safety, reputation, and belonging. Silence here is not neutrality. It is shaped by power.

What happens in Mira's body in that moment is not only about emotion. It is about history, risk, and survival. Her body is responding to conditions it has learned to read long before language steps in.

This chapter is about learning to notice the kinds of moments that Mira and each and every one of us experience; not to correct them, but to understand how systems come to live inside posture, breath, tension, collapse, and hesitation. The practices are not being offered as ways to privately cope with these conditions. They are offered as ways to notice how these conditions already live in the body, so that what has been carried in silence, adaptation, vigilance, or withdrawal is no longer misread as personal failure. What becomes visible in this way may support protection, strategy, refusal, boundary making, or collective recognition. It does not have to become explanation, disclosure, or performance in order to matter.

The practices in this chapter are intentionally offered to be regular, repeatable practices. They are not designed as one-time exercises to complete and move past—they are meant to be returned to over time. You may practice alone or with others. You may practice regularly, occasionally, or not at all on some days. Whatever you choose is valid. When you are ready, we would encourage you to find others with whom you can share this journey. The practices are especially supportive when done in collective spaces, where shared presence can offer a different kind of safety, clarify how power moves between bodies, and support both individual and collective liberatory hopes. You may choose to form a small practice group with people you are reading this workbook with, or you may join Pause for Perspective's mindfulness sangha, which meets regularly (weekly or bi-weekly, depending on the cycle), as an ongoing collective space for practice and reflection. While not a requirement, group practice is aligned with the ethics of this work, which understands safety, care, and liberation as co-held rather than individual trials.

Further, you are also not required to move through this chapter, and forthcoming ones, in sequence. You may return to these practices slowly over time, moving back and forth between chapters and practices. You may also skip this chapter entirely for now and begin with the next chapters which explore practices related to the Body as a Site of Liberation, Resistance, and Protest; you can return here later if, and when, these practices feel accessible or relevant. There is no correct order with this chapter particularly. Your body, your context, and your life circumstances decide the rhythm of this work.

As you enter these practices, it is important to know that you always retain choice. You may pass, pause, change posture, adapt a practice, or stop entirely at any point. You never owe yourself "depth," "insight," "emotional exposure," "calm," or "transformation." These practices do not ask your body to perform or produce anything.

Safety in this work is structural and relational, not merely internal. Caste, race, class, gender, disability, neurodivergence, sexuality, language, housing, food security, and medical access shape how easily the body can soften, slow down, or turn inward. Some bodies arrive with more ease. Others arrive with bracing or collapse. All of this belongs here.

Moreover, turning inward is never required. For many trauma-impacted, neurodivergent, disabled, queer, trans, Dalit, Bahujan, and Adivasi bodies, inward attention may feel unsafe or overwhelming. This reflects lived history and present conditions, not personal limitation. Sensing from the outside through sound, texture, visual focus, movement, rocking, stimming, pressure, or relational presence is always valid. Further, stillness is not superior to movement and silence is not more meaningful than sound. These are all legitimate bodily languages.

Ultimately, your capacity determines the pace, and capacity changes from day to day. Slowing down, stepping back, or stopping are all forms of consent. Discomfort, numbness, shutdown, vigilance, distraction, and confusion are forms of bodily communication, not failures of practice.

These practices do not aim to regulate, fix, or improve the body. They begin with recognition of how the body has learned to survive, adapt, refuse, and protect. Recognition is the ground from which choice, dignity, and possibility slowly become available. With this orientation in place, we begin with a practice that supports noticing where history, protection, and possibility live in the body.

Further, you may already have many ways your body responds, protects, pauses, reaches, withdraws, and settles without any formal practice. The breath changes when there is relief. The shoulders lift under pressure. The body pulls back before a boundary is crossed. These are not created by mindfulness. They are forms of embodied knowing that already live in you. The practices in this workbook offer space around what is already happening. When done on your own or with others, they support a slowing down to notice and make visible what is usually private. In that way, the practices perhaps shape your relationship with the body you already have.

In this chapter, the four practices you are about to meet are being held in relation to the ethics that shape this workbook. They come from traditional Mindfulness Based Interventions (MBIs) and from the original Mindfulness Based Symptom Management program,[6] an ethics-based mindfulness program that uses embodied practices and five skillful habits to help people notice, stay with, and respond to their experiences with greater clarity, care, and agency. Within the frame of embodied social justice

- *Body Scan* can sometimes become a way of noticing how safety, threat, and history are mapped across the body, which may open toward experiences of aliveness and choice that this work associates with liberation.
- *Awareness of Breath* may make more visible how attention moves under pressure and permission, which for some bodies can reveal forms of protest such as fatigue, vigilance, or refusal to perform.
- The *BEST (Body, Emotion, Sensations, and Thoughts)* practice may support staying with the complexity of experience without immediately splitting it into parts that must be fixed, which this work understands as one possible form of resistance to urgency and self-surveillance.
- *Loving Kindness* can be approached here as an ethical widening of care that does not deny harm or inequality, while still insisting on dignity as a shared condition of life.

It is important to acknowledge that these practice intentions are not guarantees or outcomes that everyone will experience. They are ways that these practices are offered within an embodied social justice frame, with full recognition that bodies respond differently based on history, access, safety, and social location.

For all four practices, if you are sharing the practice out loud, or reading it for yourself or a group, you may let the sentences move at a pace your body can stay with. For some, one natural breath may offer a rhythm for each sentence. For others, a gentle count of a few seconds, sometimes five, sometimes longer, may offer another way of slowing the pace.

Practice Invitation 1: Body Scan

A practice for noticing where history, protection, and possibility live in the body

As you step into this first practice of the chapter, you are not beginning something new so much as deepening the listening you have already been doing. The *Body Scan* offers a slow, spacious way to notice how different regions of your body hold sensation, memory, protection, and possibility. It does not ask you to find anything specific or to stay with anything that feels too close. It simply invites you to meet the body as it is today, with the understanding that what you notice now is shaped by the worlds you live(d) in.

This practice supports you to gently notice how different parts of your body hold sensation, protection, fatigue, vigilance, ease, or quiet. It is not about scanning for problems. It is about knowing the language your body already speaks.

Arriving

You may lie down, sit, stand, lean, or move gently.
Let your eyes be open or soft.
If it feels supportive, you may let your body settle into whatever is holding you.
If settling does not feel safe, staying alert, moving, or keeping your eyes open are equally valid ways of being here.

You are not required to be still.
There is nothing you need to do well.

Choosing an Anchor

You may begin by noticing the in-breath and the out-breath as they naturally arrive, or you may choose another steady sensation such as sound, contact of your body or part of your body with another surface, temperature, pressure, or gentle movement.

There is no preferred anchor. You may return to your chosen anchor at any time.

Name your anchor: ____

You may also choose to use one or both hands as support at any point in this practice. Placing a hand on a part of the body can offer steadiness, warmth, or clearer sensing. This is an option, not a requirement.

Breath as Entry (If Breath Is Your Anchor)

If the breath feels available, you might notice:

- the belly rising and falling
- the chest expanding and softening
- or the breath simply as a quiet rhythm

On each out-breath, you may sense a small letting go.
Not forcing heaviness.
Just allowing.

Pause for three natural breaths.

Moving Through the Body

You do not need to follow the full sequence of the body. You may stay with one region, return to your anchor, or move ahead in the scan at any point. Skipping is always allowed.

Lower Body

When you feel ready, let your attention move to the toes of one foot.

If it feels supportive, you may rest a hand here as you notice this region.

You may imagine the breath moving gently down into the toes on the in-breath, and on the out-breath imagine it moving back up.

Or you may simply notice whatever sensation is present.
Notice pressure, pulsing, numbness, temperature, tingling, or blankness.
Whatever is here is enough.

[Pause instructions for three breaths.]

Let your attention move to:

- the bottom of the foot
- the heel
- the ankle
- the lower leg, the shin, and calf
- the knee and the thigh

You may breathe into each region, observe it as it is, or keep a hand there as support.

[Pause instructions for three breaths.]

Now the other leg, in the same way.
Toes, foot, ankle, lower leg, knee, thigh.

[Pause instructions for three breaths.]

Pelvis and Back

Let awareness move through the hips and pelvis.
Notice the contact with the surface beneath you.
If it feels supportive, a hand here is optional support.

You may imagine the breath filling this whole region.

[Pause instructions for three breaths.]

Now the lower back.
Then the upper back.
You may notice movement in the ribcage with the breath.
You may rest a hand on the back or ribs if that helps you stay connected.

[Pause instructions for three breaths.]

Belly and Chest

Let attention move to the belly.
Rising and falling.
If it feels steadying, you may place a hand here.

Then to the chest.
You may notice the movement of the lungs or the beating of the heart.
Place a hand here if it offers support.

[Pause instructions for three breaths.]

Arms and Hands

If you have been using your hands as support elsewhere in the body, you may now bring attention back to them, or you may continue to rest them wherever they feel needed.

Now, bring attention to the fingertips of both hands together.
Notice warmth, tingling, vibration, or stillness.
Let attention move through:

- the palms
- the backs of the hands
- the wrists
- the forearms
- the elbows
- the upper arms

Now the shoulders.
Many bodies carry responsibility, vigilance, and fatigue here.
You may rest one or both hands on the shoulders if that feels supportive.

[Pause instructions for three breaths.]

Neck, Face, and Head

Let awareness move to the neck.
Notice swallowing, air moving, or subtle holding.
You may support this area with a hand if that feels grounding.
Then the jaw, the lips, the mouth, the tongue.
Then the nose, the eyes, the temples, the ears.
You may notice tension in the forehead.
If it feels supportive, allow the forehead to soften slightly.
If not, simply notice what is here.
Now the back of the head.
And the top of the head.

[Pause instructions for three breaths.]

Whole Body (If This Feels Possible)

Some bodies sense most clearly through contact and pressure. If using your hands has helped you feel more present or more protected, that is already part of whole-body awareness.

> If it feels possible, you may imagine the breath moving through the whole body, from the top of the head down through the spine and out through the feet.
> You may sense the body as one whole field of experience.
> If the body feels scattered, distant, uneven, or segmented, that way of sensing is also complete.
> You are not trying to reach a particular state.

[Pause instructions for three breaths.]

Returning

> Slowly begin to re-orient to the room.
> You may wiggle your fingers or toes.
> Notice sounds.
> Notice light.

If you are with others, you may take a few moments of shared quiet before moving on.

As you come out of the *Body Scan*, you may have noticed that some parts of your body were easier to sense than others. Some places may have felt blank, guarded, tight, heavy, or unexpectedly soft. Bodies do not organize themselves randomly. They organize in response to real conditions of safety, danger, permission, and consequence.

You might recall Mira here. When her stomach tightened and her breath shortened in the meeting room, the sensation itself was only part of the experience. The weight also came from how she had to relate to that sensation in a space where speaking carried risk. In a similar way, what you notice in your body is shaped not only by sensation, but also by the conditions under which your body learned to protect, brace, remain silent, or endure.

This does not mean the body is broken. It means the body is communicating. It has mapped where care was present and where it was not. Recognition of this is not about fixing these responses. It is about seeing how deeply they make sense. It is natural to only notice sensations and not come to a felt sense or meaning of them. It is important to notice the demand on ourselves to make meaning right away and gently offer the room our bodyminds may need to see ourselves in this way first.

Body Scan Closing Reflections

You may choose one or more question. You may skip reflection entirely.

- What did I notice most clearly in my body today?
- How did I relate to that sensation or absence of sensation?
- Did my stance toward this part of my body feel shaped by protection, pressure, silence, or survival?

- If I stay with this sensation gently for a few breaths, does anything shift in meaning or feeling?
- What does this part of my body seem to need right now, given the worlds it moves through?

Practice Invitation 2: Awareness of Breath

A practice for noticing how attention moves under pressure and permission

This practice follows the *Body Scan* by turning toward a different layer of experience. While the *Body Scan* supported noticing where sensation and protection live in the body, this practice supports noticing how attention moves when it meets something steady, repetitive, or subtle.

The breath is one possible anchor here, but it is not the only one. What matters is not training attention to behave, but recognizing how attention has been shaped by demand, vigilance, fatigue, expectation, permission, and survival.

Arriving

You may sit, stand, lie down, lean, or move gently.
You may be on a chair, a cushion, the floor, or supported in another way.
Let your arms rest wherever they feel most at ease.
You may place your hands on your lap, thighs, belly, chest, or wherever there is a sense of steadiness.

If it feels supportive, you may let the body settle into whatever is holding it.
If settling does not feel safe, staying alert, shifting position, or keeping your eyes open are equally valid ways of being here.
You do not need to hold your body in any particular way.

You may gently notice where there is strain, holding, fatigue, or comfort, and adjust as needed.

Bring an attitude of curiosity to this moment, not as a task to perform, but as a way of staying in contact with what is already here.

Choosing an Anchor

You may choose one steady point of contact for your attention. This could be:

- the natural rhythm of the breath
- the feeling of your feet on the ground
- the support of the chair, wall, or floor
- sound in the room
- temperature on the skin
- gentle rocking or repetitive movement

There is no preferred anchor.

Name your anchor: ____

You may also use one or both hands as support at any time.

A hand on the belly, chest, throat, heart, or thigh can offer steadiness, warmth, or clearer sensing.

This is always optional.

If Breath Is Your Anchor

If the breath feels available to you today, you might begin by noticing:

- the expansion of the abdomen on the in-breath
- the softening on the out-breath

You may follow this sensation for a few natural rounds of breathing.

You might notice:

- coolness as the breath comes in
- warmth as it goes out
- or no clear temperature at all

There is no need to breathe in any particular way.

You are not trying to deepen, slow, or steady the breath.
You are simply allowing the breath to breathe itself.
If at any point the breath feels uncomfortable, overwhelming, or distant, you may return to another anchor.

Following Where the Breath Is Most Noticeable

You may notice that the breath is more available in some places than others.
For some, it is most noticeable at the nostrils.
For some, in the chest.
For some, in the belly.
For some, it may not feel clearly located anywhere at all.
Wherever the breath is most noticeable is enough.
You may follow it there for a few moments.

Noticing Wandering

At times, your attention may stay with the anchor.
At other times, it will move into thoughts, memories, images, planning, worry, blankness, sleepiness or something else

When you notice that your attention has moved, simply notice that it has wandered.
There is nothing wrong with this.
If it feels possible, you may gently guide your attention back to the anchor.
You do not need to do this perfectly.

The noticing, the leaving, and the returning are all part of the practice.

You may find it helpful to remember:
The practice is not in staying.
The practice is in noticing.

If judgment arises about how this is going, that too becomes part of what is noticed.
You may quietly bring a quality of kindness to the way you return.

Loitering with Gentleness

As the practice continues, you may begin noticing how physical sensations change with each in-breath and each out-breath.

You may notice subtle shifts, pauses. Irregularities, steadiness, or absence of sensation or something else.
You may also notice emotional or mental tones arising alongside the breath.
You do not need to follow them or push them away.

You may continue to return to the simple fact of being here with whatever is present.
If it feels steadying, you may place a hand on your body as you notice attention drifting or returning.
This is not to control attention, but to offer the body a sense of contact and presence.

Breath as Reconnecting with Being Alive

At some point, you may begin to notice the breath simply as a sign of being alive.
Not as an object to focus on.
Not as a tool for calming.
Just as a quiet movement that continues on its own.
You may sense being here, being alive, being present to yourself
If this does not arise, that is also complete.

Closing

When you feel ready, allow awareness to widen slightly.
Let sound, space, and light enter your noticing.
You may gently move your fingers or toes.
If you are practicing with others, you may take a few moments of shared quiet before moving on.

As you come out of this practice, you may begin by noticing what your attention actually did. For some, it may have stayed close to the anchor for a while. For others, it may have wandered often. It might have felt restless, foggy, effortful, sharp, avoidant, or tired. There is nothing to correct here. This is simply how attention arrived today.

You may also begin noticing how you related to that movement of attention. For some, there may have been judgment about drifting. For others, frustration, pressure, embarrassment, indifference, amusement, or resignation might have appeared. Some of you may have tried to control attention. Some may have let it come and go.

As you sense into that stance toward your attention, you might notice small shifts in the body. The chest may tighten with judgment. The shoulders may drop with relief. The belly may brace with effort. Or something else entirely may be present. Whatever you notice belongs to how this moment is being lived through the body.

Remember Mira—just as her body tightened before words could form, your attention may tighten, race, scatter, or go blank long before meaning is clear. These movements are not random. They are shaped by what your nervous system has learned is expected, demanded, punished, or required in order to belong or survive.

From here, you might explore whether a small shift in intention feels possible.
Not to hold attention perfectly.
Not to succeed at the practice.
But perhaps to meet the movement of attention with a little more curiosity or patience.

You might quietly notice:

What happens if I stop treating drifting as failure?
What if this movement is showing me fatigue instead of inadequacy?
What if vigilance is showing me care for safety rather than a flaw?

Sometimes what looks like distraction reveals a different truth entirely.

Awareness of Breath Closing Reflections

You may choose one or more question. You may write, rest, move, or skip.

- What did my attention tend to do most often during this practice?
- How did I feel toward that movement of attention?
- What showed up in how I related to myself (judgment, pressure, kindness, fatigue or something else)?
- When I softened my stance, even slightly, did the experience change in any way?
- What might my attention be protecting me from right now?

Practice Invitation 3: B-E-S-T

Body, Emotions, Sensations, and Thoughts in Conversation

This practice brings together the *Body Scan* and *Awareness of Breath*. Instead of noticing body, breath, or attention separately, *BEST* invites you to sense how Body, Emotions, Sensations, and Thoughts move together in lived experience.

There is no right order in which these arise. At times a thought leads. At times sensation leads. At times emotion arrives first. At times the body speaks before anything can be named. This practice supports recognition of these movements as they happen, without trying to organize, correct, or improve them.

Arriving

You may take a seated position on a chair, cushion, floor, or any surface that offers support.
You may also stand, lean, or shift position if sitting is not accessible.
Your eyes may be open or soft.
Let your hands rest wherever they feel most supportive.
On your lap, thighs, belly, chest, or heart.
You may change where your hands rest at any time.

If it feels supportive, you may notice the in-breath and the out-breath.
If breath does not feel accessible, you may notice contact with the floor, sound in the room, or gentle movement instead.

You are bringing yourself to this moment as you are.
You do not need to arrive in any particular state.
At the sound of a bell, or after a few steady breaths, allow your attention to gently settle where it naturally goes first.

Beginning with Breath (If Breath Is Available)

If the breath feels available, you may notice breathing in, breathing out.
You do not need to change the breath. But if that does happen just follow that as well
You may follow where the breath is most noticeable in the nostrils, chest, abdomen or nowhere clearly at all.

You may rest here for a few breaths.
If breath is not accessible, you may remain with another anchor.

B—Body

Now, gently bring awareness to the body.
You may notice posture, contact with the surface beneath you, weight, fatigue, tension, collapse, restlessness, blankness or something else.
You may place a hand on any part of the body if that offers steadiness or clearer sensing.
You do not need to seek ease or comfort.
You are only noticing what is already here.

E—Emotions

Now, gently notice if there is any emotional tone present.
This may be named clearly, such as sadness, irritation, fear, tenderness, joy, numbness or it may be unclear, shifting, or unnamed.
You do not need to explain or analyze what you feel.
You are simply noticing that an emotion, or lack of emotion, is present.
You may notice how the body responds to this emotional tone.

S—Sensations

Next, notice sensations in the body.
You may notice: tightness, warmth, cold, pressure, pulsing, ache, vibration, heaviness, lightness, or nothing clearly at all.
Sensations may shift as you notice them.
Or they may stay the same.
You do not need to make them go away or become clearer.

T—Thoughts

Now, notice thoughts.
You may become aware of words, images, memories, planning, judgments, questions, or repetitive stories.
You do not need to stop thinking.
You do not need to push thoughts away.
You may simply notice: Thoughts are happening.
If judgment arises about the thoughts, that judgment is also a thought.

Letting the Four Speak Together

For a few moments, you may allow Body, Emotions, Sensations, and Thoughts to all be present at once.
You are not trying to track them perfectly.
You are letting them be in the same space.
At times one may feel louder.
At times another may move into the background.
You may rest here as they shift.

Widening and Returning

> When you feel ready, allow awareness to widen slightly.
> Notice sound, light, and the space around you.
> You may gently move your hands, feet, or shoulders.
> If you are practicing with others, you may allow a few moments of shared quiet before moving on.

As you come out of this practice, you may begin by noticing which parts of experience were most available today. Perhaps your sensations may have been clearer than emotions. Or maybe your thoughts were louder than the body. You may have noticed strong feelings with very little language for them. Maybe you noticed many words with very little sensation underneath. There is nothing to arrange or balance here. This is simply how experience organized itself today.

You may also notice how these different parts related to one another. A sensation may have carried an emotion. A thought may have tried to explain a feeling. An emotion may have arrived without clear sensation. Or the body may have held everything quietly. None of these patterns are wrong. They reflect how your nervous system and history shape experience in this moment.

As you sense into this relating, you may notice subtle responses in the body. A settling when something feels understood. A tightening when something feels unclear. A pause when nothing needs to move. Or a sense of fatigue, relief, or fullness. All of this belongs to how your system is living inside this moment.

Cast your mind back to Mira. Just as her body, emotion, sensation, and thought all shifted together in a moment shaped by caste power, your own *BEST* constellation is shaped by the conditions under which your life has unfolded.

What you notice here is not a personal defect. It is a record of how your system has learned to survive, adapt, protest, freeze, endure, and sometimes reach for possibility. From here, you might sense whether a small shift in intention feels possible. Not to change what is present but to relate to what is present with a little more space or care.

BEST Closing Reflections

You may choose one or more question to answer. You may also skip reflection entirely.

- Which of the four felt most present for me today: body, emotions, sensations, or thoughts?
- How did I relate to what I noticed?
- Did my stance feel shaped by protection, pressure, habit, or care?
- If I soften my stance even slightly, does anything shift in how this experience feels?
- What might this constellation be protecting me from right now?

Practice Invitation 4: Loving Kindness

You may choose to sit, lie down, stand, or shift in any way that helps your body feel supported enough to stay with this practice. There is no correct posture.
Your hands may rest on your lap, your chest, your belly, or anywhere that offers steadiness. You may use touch as a way to stay connected, or not at all.
Your eyes may be open or closed.
You are not required to feel warmth, softness, or generosity for this practice to count.

Arriving

Begin by noticing that you are breathing.
Not in any special way.
Not to calm or change anything.
Just noticing that breath is moving.
If it helps, you may feel the movement of breath under your hand.
You are not asked to open your heart.
You are only invited to stay with what is already here.

Beginning with the Self

(Only if this feels possible)

If it feels safe enough today, you may begin with yourself.
You are not required to feel kindness toward yourself for this to be valid.

You may silently offer one or two of these phrases, changing the words as needed:

- May I live with as much safety as is possible right now.
- May I live with dignity, even inside constraint.
- May I have what I need to keep going.
- May I not be forced to disappear from my own life.

If these words feel unreachable, flat, irritating, or distant, that also belongs here.

This practice does not require belief.

Someone or Something That Has Offered Care

(If and when you are ready)

You may now, if it feels supportive, bring to mind someone or something that has offered you care or steadiness at some point. This could be a person, an animal, a place, a tree, a song, a teacher, an ancestor, or a memory.

You do not need to visualize clearly. A sense is enough.

You may offer:

- May you live with safety.
- May you live with dignity.
- May you have what you need.
- May you continue to be part of what makes life survivable.

Notice what happens in your body.

There is no correct response.

Staying with What Is Hard

(Without forcing care toward harm)

At this point, many loving kindness practices would invite you to bring to mind someone you struggle with. In this version of the practice, you are not required to do this.

If your body carries anger, grief, fear, withdrawal, or refusal toward someone, you are not asked to soften that.

You are not asked to reconcile.
You are not asked to forgive.
You are not asked to wish well toward anyone who has harmed you.
You are not asked to transform injustice into inner peace.
If what is present is protection, distance, or no contact, that can also be held as part of loving yourself.
You may return here to your breath or to your own body if that feels steadier.

Widening Toward Collective Life

(Without erasing power)

If it feels possible, you may now widen your attention beyond yourself.

Not toward "all beings" as an abstract ideal, but toward people living inside real conditions of inequality.

You might hold in mind:

- people under caste or race oppression
- people under surveillance or displacement
- people living with disability, pain, or medical neglect
- people surviving war, hunger, or state violence
- people whose genders, bodies, or loves are criminalized

You are not asked to take responsibility for their suffering.

You may quietly offer:

- May dignity not be erased.
- May survival not be confused with failure.
- May people not be required to disappear in order to belong.

You may include yourself here too.

Closing

Let your attention return to your body.
To the surface beneath you.
To the weight of your body where it rests.
To the movement of breathing.

You are not asked to carry this practice forward as a mandate.
You are only invited to notice that you remained in relationship with yourself for these moments.

When you are ready, you may open your eyes or shift your body.

As you come out of this practice, you may notice how it felt to offer care in different directions, or to not offer it at all. Some may have felt closeness toward themselves. Some may have felt distance, resistance, grief, or neutrality. Some may have stayed mainly with breath or with the body. There is nothing to correct here. This is how this practice met your life today.

You may also notice how your body responded as the field widened. There may have been warmth, contraction, steadiness, irritation, numbness, sadness, or very little change. All of this belongs to how care is shaped under the conditions you live in.

As this moment settles, you may sense what remains. Perhaps a trace of steadiness. Perhaps fatigue. Perhaps guardedness. Perhaps nothing in particular. Whatever is present does not need to become intention, meaning, or outcome. It is simply how this moment is being held.

Reflection Questions for the Loving Kindness Practice

You may choose one or more question to contemplate. You may also skip reflection entirely.

- As you moved through the different directions in the practice, where did your attention spend the most time?
- How did you relate to that movement of attention? With ease, pressure, distance, irritation, tenderness, effort, or something else?
- As you notice that stance, what happened in your body? Did anything soften, tighten, brace, withdraw, steady, or feel tired?
- Was there any point where you chose not to offer care? What did that choice feel like in the body?
- As you come out of the practice now, what remains in your body? Does it ask for rest, boundary, quiet, movement, or nothing in particular?

In shared practice spaces, people meet these practices in many ways: through movement, rest, sleep, listening, watching, reading aloud for others, drawing, walking, eating, music, journaling, or simply being beside another without doing the practice at all. Some arrive with curiosity, some with hesitation, some with memories or overwhelm, and learn to adapt through open eyes, movement, or distance. All of these are ways of practicing. None are deviations. They reflect how bodies seek safety, contact, rest, and dignity under different conditions.

Across this chapter, you were invited into four ways of meeting the body, not to perfect yourself or manage sensations away, but to stay with what is already unfolding and how you are meeting it. The *Body Scan* supported noticing how experience lives across the body through protection, tension, rest, and withdrawal. *Awareness of Breath* returned attention to the most ordinary rhythm of aliveness, beyond productivity or permission. *BEST* invited you to stay with experience without breaking it into parts that need fixing, and *Loving Kindness* invited care as an ethical stance shaped by unequal conditions rather than sentiment alone.

Together, these practices enact the three ethics that shape this workbook: liberation, by returning you to aliveness and choice even inside constraint; protest, by refusing the demand to override exhaustion, bypass pain, or make yourself palatable; and resistance, by staying in relationship with what is happening without surrendering to urgency, shame, productivity, or disappearance. These practices are meant to be returned to, not completed. They may be taken up alone or with others, in stillness or movement, with adaptation, with rest, or not at all on some days. You are not moving forward because you mastered them, but because you are in relationship with your body.

What may have felt familiar: the way the breath settles with relief, the way the body braces before difficulty, the steadiness of touch, are not things the practices invent. They are ways your body has already learned to live. What changes with intentional practice, alone or together, is not the presence of embodiment but the conditions around it. Embodiment here is not something to achieve, but something to keep returning to as life continues to meet you, and as these ways of sitting, noticing, touching, breathing, and offering care become the ground from which the rest of this work unfolds.

References

1. Selvan A, Nayar, S. *Embodied social justice counseling for Indian communities: Integrating theory and practice*. Taylor & Francis. 2027.
2. Haines SK. *The politics of trauma: Somatics, healing, and social justice*. North Atlantic Books. 2019.
3. Dana D. *The polyvagal theory in therapy: Engaging the rhythm of regulation*. WW Norton. 2018.
4. van der Kolk B. *The body keeps the score: Brain, mind, and body in the healing of trauma*. Viking. 2014.
5. Soundararajan T. *The trauma of caste: A Dalit feminist meditation on survivorship, healing, and abolition*. North Atlantic Books. 2022.
6. Crane RS, Kuyken W, Hastings RP, Rothwell N, Williams JMG. Training teachers to deliver mindfulness-based interventions: Learning from the UK experience. *Mindfulness* 2017;8(5):1183–1193. doi:10.1007/s12671-010-0010-9

Part II

Body as a Site of Liberation

What comes to mind when you read the phrase '*Body as a Site of Liberation*'? Draw or write your reflections in this space...

DOI: 10.4324/9781003672203-5

To speak of the Body as a Site of Liberation is not to suggest that the body is free. It is to recognize that even within conditions of deep constraint, the body continues to sense, respond, refuse, adapt, seek, brace, soften, withdraw, and reach. Liberation in this framing is not an outcome. It is not something achieved after oppression is dismantled. It is the ongoing, often fragile, often interrupted capacity to remain in relationship with aliveness inside conditions that attempt to regulate, erase, discipline, exhaust, or disappear certain bodies.

In dominant therapeutic and spiritual traditions, liberation is often imagined as transcendence. One is encouraged to rise above pain, detach from identity, override the body, or regulate distress into calm as a striving to achieve. In this workbook, liberation is understood differently. Liberation is not about a spiritual idea of relinquishing or rising above the body; rather, it is seen as a process of knowing the body as responding to the world. It is not about becoming unaffected by harm. It is about recognizing how harm and survival already live in sensation, posture, breath, movement, collapse, vigilance, fatigue, pleasure, and want.

Bodies do not encounter the world as blank slates. They are shaped by caste hierarchies, gendered surveillance, compulsory able-bodiedness, psychiatric norms, racialized control, state violence, economic extraction, and the everyday risks carried by queer, trans, disabled, neurodivergent, and caste-oppressed lives. As a result, aliveness is not equally protected. Rest is not equally available. Visibility is not equally safe. Silence is not equally chosen. What may look like withdrawal in one context may be the only available form of self-protection in another. What may look like passivity may be the body refusing conditions that have already proven dangerous.

To name the Body as a Site of Liberation is to refuse the idea that freedom only lives in thought, intention, or future political change. It is to notice that even within surveillance and scarcity, the body continues to register warmth, constriction, rhythm, overwhelm, relief, irritation, curiosity, hunger, pleasure, and the pull toward or away from contact. These small, ordinary signals are significant. They are the raw materials through which people orient toward dignity, safety, distance, connection, and direction.

In many dominant frameworks, the body is approached as something to be corrected. It is regulated, trained, disciplined, medicated, optimized, and reformed in the name of productivity, wellness, functionality, or normalcy. In contrast, the work you do in this book begins with the understanding that bodies already hold intelligence shaped by history. What shows up in sensation is never only personal. Tightness in the chest, bracing in the belly, collapse in the shoulders, vigilance in the eyes, fatigue in the limbs—they all carry stories of classrooms, clinics, homes, workplaces, streets, and institutions. These are not signs of individual failure. They are traces of what the body has had to do to survive.

Liberation, in this framing, does not require that the body become calm, coherent, or consistent. It does not require that pain resolve into peace. Liberation includes the right to shake, to withdraw, to say no, to move erratically, to dissociate, to freeze, to rest, to stim, to repeat, to change one's mind, to need support, to choose distance, and, always, to return again. Liberation includes the right to have a body that is contradictory, fatigued, desiring, uncertain, and alive.

Understanding the Body as a Site of Liberation in this way is deeply shaped by disability justice and neurodivergent affirmations that challenge the idea that there is one correct way to attend, regulate, focus, move, or be still. It is shaped by Anti-Caste analysis that names how dignity, space, labor, silence, and voice are differentially distributed. It is shaped by queer and trans realities that show how safety in public space is negotiated moment by moment through posture, tone, breath, and visibility. It is shaped by narrative practices that understand people as responding to stories not of their own making; and yet still finding ways to re-author meaning and preferred possibilities.

In this framework, liberation is not a moral achievement. It is not something one earns through insight, discipline, positivity, or transcendence. It is something that flickers and fades, strengthens and retreats, depending on context, resources, risk, companionship, and time. Liberation may appear for a moment as a fuller breath after holding it too long. It may appear as the refusal to speak when speech would cost too much. It may appear as the decision to rest when productivity is demanded. It may appear as pleasure that survives despite threat. It may appear as the quiet decision to continue.

To approach the Body as a Site of Liberation is, therefore, to approach it with curiosity, respect, and political awareness (an awareness that the body is shaped by caste, race, gender, class, disability, sexuality, and other structures of power, and that what becomes possible or constrained in the body is never separate from these conditions). It is to understand that what the body is doing now is in response to and inside the conditions it has been given. To notice its call for collective and personal safety, belonging and dignity.

Chapter 4

I Am Alive!

Whether or not we name it this way, our bodies are always responding. The way attention tightens or softens. The way breath shortens or deepens. The way we withdraw, comply, confront, freeze, reach out, or stay silent. These are not neutral reactions. They are responses shaped inside caste hierarchies, psychiatric power, gendered surveillance, economic extraction, and histories of harm and belonging.

Aliveness, in this sense, is not only about feeling that something is happening. It is also about noticing how the body has learned to respond again and again. Where are our daily bodily responses being shaped toward disappearance, over-functioning, self-erasure, or adaptation to injustice? And where are they slowly reorganizing towards saying no, staying present, setting limits, seeking support, or acting in alignment with what we care about?

Sensations change. Reactions and responses shift. What feels fixed one day may loosen on another. By tracking this movement with curiosity rather than judgment, the body begins to reveal not only how oppression is lived, but also how protest gathers, how values take shape, and how the direction of one's life can quietly begin to move in the direction of our collective hopes and dreams.

In this chapter, "I Am Alive" names this living, shifting field where harm, protection, hope, capacity, refusal, and longing move together through the body. It moves from a conceptual framing of Body as a Site of Liberation into practice. It does not attempt to prove liberation. It simply invites you to notice how aliveness already appears, in small and ordinary ways, even inside constraint. Liberation here begins at the level of sensation, movement, and capacity. It begins when the body is no longer treated as a problem to be solved or a machine to be optimized. It begins when the body is met as a living record of both harm and survival.

In this chapter, aliveness is explored through four interlinked movements: sensing that the body is already responding, interrupting urgency, allowing movement to be non-normative, and noticing what the body can and cannot receive under pressure. These are not techniques for perfecting yourself. They are ways of staying in relationship with the body as it already is. From this relationship, what one wants for themselves and their collective may take shape, and/or perhaps protest and resistance takes a clearer shape. But here, the work is simpler and more difficult at the same time: **to let the body register that it is here, and that it is still responding.**

DOI: 10.4324/9781003672203-6

Gentle Orientation: Many Ways of Arriving

In this part of the workbook, we invite you to notice aliveness as it is already moving in you. Not as a goal to reach. Not as a state to maintain. But as something that shows up in small, uneven, ordinary ways.

There is no single way to practice what is offered here.

Some people will sit or lie down. Some will stand, pace, rock, stretch, or fidget. Some will listen closely. Some will drift in and out. Some will feel nothing at first. Some will feel too much in groups. Some will read the practices aloud for others and find that offering the words becomes the practice. Some will only listen to the reflections of others before trying anything themselves. Some will choose not to *do* a practice at all and instead draw, walk, eat, hum, or rest beside someone. Some may experience memories, strong emotions, or bodily reactions and need to keep their eyes open, move their body, or stay connected to the room.

All of these are ways of practicing. None of them are deviations.

Bodies shaped by caste violence, psychiatric control, ableism, gendered surveillance, poverty, migration, queerness, and chronic stress do not arrive into practice in the same way. Your body carries its own history of what has been safe, what has been demanded, what has been punished, and what has been allowed. This workbook does not ask you to override that history in the name of growth. It invites you to practice in a way that honors how your body already knows how to survive, adapt, resist, and stay.

You may choose to practice alone or with others. You may create small groups with people you are reading this workbook with. You may also choose to practice in community spaces such as Pause for Perspective's mindfulness sangha that meets regularly each month. Practicing together can sometimes make visible what is usually carried alone. Practicing alone can sometimes make space for what has never been witnessed before. Neither is better. Both are forms of collective life.

You do not need to move through all the practices in this chapter. You may return to just one practice again and again. You may skip this chapter entirely and come back later. Perhaps Chapter 6—Freeze as Protest—may be a chapter that you feel moved to partake in if difficult experiences, potentially experiences of oppression or trauma, come to the surface often. You may move back and forth between this current chapter and the following chapter or other chapters. The workbook is meant to adapt around your body, not the other way around.

It is also possible that as you begin, you will recognize that you already have embodied ways of doing what these practices point towards. The way your breath settles when there is a small moment of relief. The way your body braces before something difficult. The way movement, repetition, stillness, touch, sound, or withdrawal already help you get through the day. These practices do not create embodiment. They offer conditions to notice, shape, and stay in relationship with what your body is already doing to live.

You are always invited to pause, pass, stop, adapt, or return later. Safety here is not a personal achievement. It is something that is co-held through pacing, choice, structure, and relationship. *What can you think of right now that would help you pause, adapt, and hold safety in your practice?* Jot down your ideas below:

Practice Invitation 1: Sensing the Pulse of Aliveness

This practice begins before you do anything on purpose

It begins in the moment your body hears these words and starts to respond. Perhaps you notice a subtle tightening at the thought of 'practice.' Perhaps there is a wish to sit properly. Perhaps a resistance to sitting at all. Perhaps an ache draws your attention. Perhaps the body wants to move, stretch, lie down, or look away. Perhaps there is a familiar pressure to 'do this right,' or a tiredness that wants nothing more.

All of this is already the pulse of aliveness.

Aliveness here does not mean comfort, clarity, or calm. It means that your body is responding to what is being asked of it right now. Even aversion is a response. Even distraction is a response. Even the wish to change what is happening is a response. Even the urge to push sensation away is a response shaped by how the body has learned to be in discomfort, demand, scrutiny, and expectation. This practice does not try to correct any of these movements. It invites you to let them be part of what you notice.

You may choose any position that feels supportive enough right now. Remember, even the process of choosing is part of the practice. You may sit, lie down, stand, pace, lean, curl up, or keep moving. You may notice a pull towards stillness or a pull towards motion. Your eyes may open or close on their own. You may feel drawn to place a hand on your body, or you may feel resistant to touch. You may already be adjusting in small ways to lessen effort, avoid strain, or seek steadiness. Those adjustments are not interruptions. They are the body signaling what it needs.

You may also notice thoughts like:

- "This is not working."
- "I should feel something by now."
- "My body hurts too much for this."
- "I don't want to be here."
- "I want this to stop."

Or other thoughts. *Write these down here as they come to mind…*

These too belong to the pulse of aliveness. They carry information about pressure, fear, fatigue, hope, or past learning. Nothing here needs to be pushed away for the practice to continue.

If following these words ever feels too much, you may simply stay with this single orientation, in whatever way is possible: "*Something is happening in my body right now.*"

You do not need to locate it.
You do not need to understand it.
You do not need to like it.

The Practice

For a few moments, you might begin by noticing that you are here.

Noticing contact with the ground, a chair, a wall, your own hands, or the air around you.

You may notice breath if that feels accessible, but there is no need to focus on it. You might instead notice temperature, pressure, movement, stillness, or the impulse to change position.

Then, very gently, you might ask yourself, without needing to answer in words:

> *Where, if anywhere, do I sense even a small signal more than another, or perhaps in a chorus, that something is alive in me right now?*

It might be a pulsing, a stretch, a flutter, a tightening, a warmth, a sigh, a restlessness, a dull ache, your breath, or nothing in particular.

You do not need to search.
You do not need to interpret.
You are not trying to make anything happen.
You are noticing what is already responding.

If your attention wanders, that is part of what is happening.

If you want to stop, change how you are doing this, or not do it at all, that too is part of what is happening. Allow yourself to shift if you are moved to do so.

You might stay with this noticing for a few breaths, a minute, or longer if that feels okay.

When you are ready, you can let this specific noticing soften, while remaining in the room, in your body, in your own way.

Reflection Questions

You may choose one or more of the following questions. You may also skip reflection entirely.

1 Where did your attention spend most of its time during this practice?
2 How did you relate to what you noticed: With curiosity, effort, doubt, irritation, distance, tenderness, or something else?

3 As you notice that stance now, what do you sense in your body?
4 Was there any moment when you wanted to stop, change how you were doing the practice, or not do it at all?
5 Do any of your bodily responses today feel shaped by what you have had to adapt to in order to be safe, accepted, or productive?
6 As you come out of the practice now, what remains most present?

Lived Experience: Maya

When Maya first encountered this practice, they noticed their body reacting before they had even decided whether to participate. Their shoulders lifted slightly at the word *practice*. Their eyes scanned the room. Their jaw tightened. A familiar readiness moved through their body. This was not a failure to arrive. This was the body arriving exactly as it had learned to arrive in spaces where it did not feel fully free to rest.

Maya is queer. Much of their early aliveness had been shaped inside vigilance. Public spaces required alertness. Conversations required calibration. The body learned to stay partly braced, partly watchful, even in moments that were meant to be ordinary. Over time, this bracing became so familiar that it began to feel like stillness.

As they listened to the invitation to choose any position, Maya noticed irritation arise. Part of them wanted to lie down. Another part did not trust that wanting.

They stayed seated, feet tucked under the chair, hands gripping the edges without realizing it. Only later did they notice the effort in their arms. When the suggestion came to simply notice where the body was already responding, Maya felt a flicker of confusion. Responding to what? The room was quiet. Nothing was happening. And yet, their foot was tapping. Their breath was shallow. Their eyes kept opening even when they meant to close them.

That was when it landed: *this is the practice.*

Maya did not suddenly relax. Their body did not soften all at once. But for the first time, they noticed that vigilance itself was a form of aliveness. Not something to get rid of. Something to understand.

Over weeks of returning to this kind of noticing, Maya began to sense that their body no longer responded in exactly the same way in every space. In some rooms, the breath returned sooner. In some conversations, the shoulders did not lift as high. In moments of shared laughter, the body stayed present a few seconds longer before preparing to retreat. For Maya, "I Am Alive" did not begin to mean that danger had disappeared. It began to mean that the body was no longer limited to one survival pattern. It meant that what once felt fixed as bracing now had small edges of movement.

These shifts were not private achievements. They were shaped by access to queer-affirming spaces, by being in rooms where names were not questioned, where bodies were not explained, where vigilance could be shared rather than carried alone. Each moment of aliveness carried quiet information about what kinds of worlds make breathing more possible.

Maya also noticed that when the body was not fully collapsed into alertness, something else became available. There was more room to say no. More room to leave. More room to stay and resist. More room to imagine change beyond the self. Aliveness did not replace struggle. It changed how struggle could be held.

In the practice, Maya noticed that aliveness did not always arrive as energy or joy. Sometimes it arrived as irritation that refused to be smoothed over. Sometimes as grief that could finally be felt without shutting down. Sometimes as the simple decision to rest instead of pushing through. Each of these became part of how their body participated in widening the conditions under which queer lives can breathe. For Maya, "I Am Alive" was no longer a declaration of arrival. It became a moving relationship with the world, shaped by who was present, what was permitted, what was contested, and what was slowly being built together.

This practice does not define liberation as ease or confidence. It understands liberation as noticing how the body responds under different conditions. Many bodies shaped by caste or race violence, queerphobia, disability stigma, surveillance, or chronic precarity respond in ways that are deeply learned and protective. To notice these responses, without demanding that they change, is already a refusal of systems that expect us to override ourselves.

Sometimes, what we notice is that the body does not always respond in one fixed way. Even within constraint, different contexts evoke different sensations, impulses, and possibilities. This variability is not a sign of progress; it is simply part of how aliveness moves.

As conditions of safety, recognition, and collective care shift, we may find more spaces where what we truly want feels possible. And even when those conditions are absent, sensing what matters—what the body signals as important—is itself a form of aliveness. These moments are not achievements. They are glimpses into the kinds of worlds that support us.

Liberation here is not something to reach. It is the ongoing practice of noticing how the body responds to the world and what those responses reveal about our values, our longing, and our connection to collective life.

Practice Invitation 2: Mindfulness Bell

This practice is an invitation to interrupt urgency without demanding the body become calm. The bell is not used as a tool for control. It is used as a pause that makes room for noticing how the body is already responding in the middle of movement, work, conversation, or withdrawal.

For many of us, urgency is not a personal habit. It is produced by caste pressure, productivity demands, gendered expectations, economic precarity, and the constant threat of being corrected, excluded, or left behind. Under these conditions, the body learns to stay ahead of rest, ahead of feeling, ahead of need. This practice does not try to undo that learning. It simply creates a small interruption where the body can be felt again as it is.

> This is a practice of liberation because it refuses the idea that attention must always be useful.
> It is a practice of protest because it interrupts the pace that keeps many bodies extractable.
> It is a practice of resistance because it reclaims brief moments of time that are not organized by demand.

The 'bell' here is not limited to sound. It refers to any moment of contact that gently interrupts automatic doing—it could be a color you choose to pause at, the sensation of a warm cup in your hands, the feeling of your feet on the cool floor, the sight of a tree, the hum of traffic or anything else. The bell is *whatever lets you arrive in the middle of your real life*.

Many bodies live under pace, surveillance, and pressure that make stopping unsafe or impossible. Thus, the bell here does not ask you to stop. It asks you only to *notice*.

> This practice becomes a form of liberation because you are reclaiming moments of contact that are usually swallowed by urgency—not to regulate but to register what is happening.
> It becomes a form of protest because urgency is a tool of oppressive systems.
> It becomes a form of resistance because it offers you a moment that does not belong to extraction.

The Practice

Choose one cue for the day (or a week or whatever duration feels right for experimentation). It could be a color, the traffic signal, your bottle of water that you take along with you throughout the day, or something else.

Name your chosen cue: ______________________________

You are invited to pause for just a moment. Not to empty the mind. Not to regulate yourself. Just to notice.

You might notice:

- where your attention was just before the bell
- what your body was doing
- whether anything shifts when you pause

You are not required to breathe in any particular way. You are not required to change your posture. You are not required to stay with the sound until it fades. You can notice for a second, or for several breaths, or not at all.

When the pause ends, you simply return to what you were doing.

This practice can be repeated many times in a day, or not at all. It can live inside classrooms, homes, clinics, kitchens, streets, buses, and waiting rooms.

Post-Practice Inquiry

You may choose one or more question. You may also skip reflection entirely.

1 Where was your attention just before the bell or pause?
2 How did you relate to the interruption: With irritation, relief, indifference, curiosity, resistance, or something else?
3 As you notice that stance now, what do you sense in your body?
4 Was there any impulse to hurry back, to stretch the pause, or to avoid it altogether?
5 What, if anything, remains?
6 In the context you live in, what might it cost your body to pause like this? And what might it protect?

____
____
____
____
____
____
____
____
____

Lived Experience: Meena

In Meena's home, evenings move quickly. Dinner has to be cooked. Homework has to be completed. Calls from relatives arrive without warning. Noise builds. Everyone is tired, and no one quite rests. Urgency is not announced. It is inherited. When Meena first heard about using a bell as a pause in a group, it felt unrealistic. There was no quiet in her house to pause into.

One evening, without naming it as a practice, she tried it. In the middle of a tense moment between her and her teenage son, with voices rising and plates still on the counter, she rang a soft bell sound on her phone. The sound startled everyone. Her son laughed. Her mother-in-law asked what she was doing. The moment broke, but not into calm. Into confusion.

Nothing transformed that night. The argument returned. The noise returned. The tasks remained. But Meena noticed something small in her body. For the first time in weeks, she felt the urge to stop without immediately explaining herself. The bell did not solve the conflict. It gave her a second to sit down.

Over the next few weeks, the bell appeared again in uneven ways. Sometimes her son rang it during homework when frustration overflowed. Sometimes Meena rang it when her body felt close to snapping. Sometimes no one rang it at all. Some days the pause led to quieter voices. Some days it only revealed how exhausted everyone already was. Some days the bell felt irritating. Some days it felt like relief. None of this followed a pattern.

The bell did not become a rule in the house. It became a question that returned from time to time: *can we stop right now without everything falling apart?* Some days, the answer was yes. Some days, it was no.

For Meena, aliveness here did not arrive as peace. It arrived as the growing recognition that stopping, even briefly, was something she and her son could begin to sense and ask for together. The pause slowly became a way of noticing whether urgency had to run the house at all times, or whether there could be moments when its grip loosened.

In many families, urgency is not chosen. Women's bodies, children's bodies, and disabled or neurodivergent bodies often carry the weight of keeping things moving, holding things together, and absorbing strain without pause. Stopping can feel irresponsible, disrespectful, or dangerous. In this context, the bell is not a tool for calm. It becomes a way of quietly questioning who gets to rest, who gets to interrupt, and whose exhaustion is allowed to matter.

Meena's use of the bell does not create harmony. It tests whether stopping can exist at all inside a structure shaped by obligation, hierarchy, and emotional labor. Each uneven pause becomes a small refusal of the idea that care must always look like endurance. When her son begins to use the bell too, the pause shifts from something Meena tries alone into a shared sensing of pace and pressure.

Liberation here does not appear as freedom from conflict. It appears as a widening of what becomes *nameable* inside conflict. The practice does not remove structural strain from family life but makes space to notice how that strain moves through bodies, and whether it must always be absorbed in the same ways. Over time, these moments of stopping can begin to change how urgency, authority, and care are held together—not all at once, and not without friction.

Practice Invitation 3: Mindful Activity

Many people are introduced to mindfulness through stillness. But stillness is not universal or neutral. Some bodies stay in contact through movement, repetition, sound, touch, pacing, rocking, or ongoing activity. For bodies shaped by caste or race oppression, disability, neurodivergence, and economic precarity, these ways of staying present emerge in conditions of crowding, surveillance, and uneven access to rest. Presence, here, is not learned through quiet alone, but through how the body moves with what is required of it.

This practice invites you to bring gentle attention into an ordinary activity that already belongs to your life. Not to improve it. Not to make it productive. Not to turn it into a performance. Only to notice how aliveness moves when the body is already in motion.

This is not about slowing everything down. It is about noticing what is already happening while you do what you already do.

Choosing an Activity

You may choose any activity that is available to you right now. For example, washing a cup, sweeping, folding clothes, cooking, walking, rocking, brushing hair, writing, watering plants, stretching, pacing, sorting objects or something else.

You are welcome to choose an activity that is usually rushed, invisible, or taken for granted. You are also welcome to choose something that already feels pleasurable or grounding.

There is no correct choice.

Name your chosen activity: ____

You may begin the activity as you normally would.

You may pause at any point. You may change the activity midway. You may stop early. You may not finish it at all.
Nothing needs to be completed for this to 'count.'

The Practice

As you move into the activity, you might begin by simply noticing that your body is doing something. You may notice how your weight shifts, how your hands move, how your breath changes, where there is effort, where there is ease, where there is irritation, where there is habit, where there is restlessness.

You do not need to make the movement smooth or slow unless your body wants that. You do not need to hold attention continuously. Attention may come and go. Each return is enough.
You are letting the activity show you how your body already knows how to move through the world.

If judgment appears, that is part of what is happening.
If distraction appears, that is part of what is happening.
If boredom, grief, pleasure, anger, fatigue, or relief appear, that is part of what is happening.

You may stay with this noticing for a short time or for the length of the activity.
When you are ready, you can let go of the specific noticing and continue or stop as feels right.

Post-Practice Inquiry

1 What did your attention naturally move toward while you were doing the activity?
2 How did you relate to the activity: With effort, resistance, tenderness, hurry, pride, boredom, curiosity, or something else?
3 As you notice that stance now, what do you sense in your body?
4 Did this activity feel chosen, required, habitual, meaningful, burdensome, or mixed?
5 Where did you notice your movement being shaped by expectations of productivity, ability, gender, or "doing it right" or something else?
6 What remains with you from this brief period of noticing?

Lived Experience: Anaya

Anaya's body rarely stays still. They rock when they think. They pace when they feel overwhelmed. They line up objects on their desk and rearrange them again and again. For years, these movements were interrupted, corrected, or teased. At school, they were told to "sit properly." At home, they were asked "Why can't you just relax?" Even in therapy spaces, the movements were sometimes treated as habits to reduce.

When Anaya encountered mindful activity, they chose pacing. Not walking for fitness. Not walking for focus. Just pacing the length of their room, back and forth, back and forth. At first, they felt self-conscious even when alone. A voice in their head said they should sit, be still, do it *properly*.

But as they stayed with the pacing, something shifted. They noticed how their breath settled into the rhythm of their steps. How their shoulders dropped when their arms swung freely. How their thoughts came in waves rather than crashing all at once. The movement was not helping them concentrate in a neat way. It was helping their body feel less trapped. Over time, Anaya began to notice that some days they rocked more, some days they paced less, some days they lined objects in careful rows, and some days they didn't need to do any of it. The practice did not turn their movements into a technique. It helped them listen to when their body needed repetition and when it wanted something else.

For Anaya, "I Am Alive" did not show up as calm. It showed up as permission. Permission for their body to move in the ways it had always known how to move, without apology. The movements did not disappear. What changed was that they no longer felt like symptoms to hide. They felt like ways of staying connected to themselves in a world that had often asked them to contain, quieten, or justify their way of being.

For many neurodivergent and queer bodies, movement that soothes or organizes the nervous system is often labeled as excess, immaturity, or dysfunction. Repetition, pacing, rocking, humming, tapping, rearranging, and looping are frequently treated as behaviors to reduce rather than ways of staying alive inside environments that overwhelm, surveil, or constrain.

This practice refuses the demand that regulation must look still, quiet, or socially acceptable. By bringing attention into the movements the body already chooses, the body is no longer forced to earn its right to move. Aliveness here is not performed as composure. It is claimed as legitimacy.

When such movements are recognized rather than corrected, the body is not required to disappear in order to belong. This does not erase the structural conditions that make containment necessary. It makes visible the intelligence the body has already developed to survive those conditions. Over time, this recognition can shift how people advocate for their needs, choose their environments, and build spaces where different rhythms of being alive are not merely tolerated but welcomed.

Practice Invitation 4: The Goblet

This practice invites you to notice how your body meets the present moment when things are moving quickly, when there is pressure to decide, respond, perform, or hold things together. It does not ask you to become calm. It does not ask you to respond well. It simply offers a way to return to what is already happening in your body, without needing to resolve it (Figure 2).

> The Goblet is shaped like what it is named after.
> A cup that receives. A narrow flute that focuses. A base that holds.
> These are not steps to master.
> They are ways the body already knows how to know its capacity,
> especially in moments that feel overwhelming or charged.

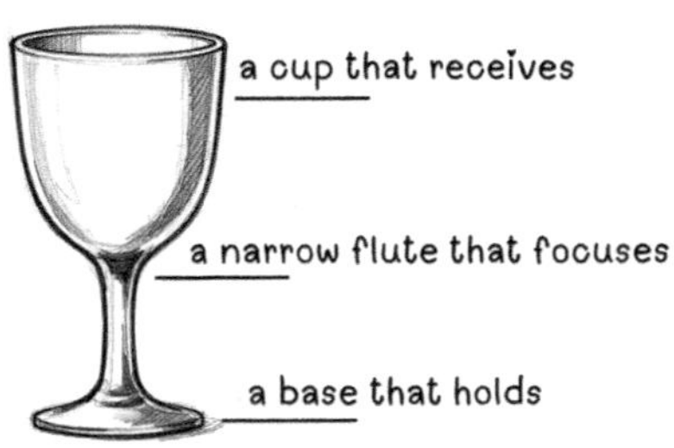

Figure 2 Goblet.

Capacity is not just an individual trait. It is shaped by caste, race, class, gender, disability, queerness, labor conditions, and relational safety. Some bodies are expected to receive far more than they have capacity for, while others are protected from having to receive at all.

It is a way of sensing what your body is already receiving, what it is still trying to hold, and where its limit appears. For many people living inside caste surveillance, gendered expectations, capitalist pace, or neurotypical norms, the body is asked to take in more than it has capacity for. The Cup shows what has already entered in the moment of practice. The Flute reveals what can be filtered or softened. The Base reminds you of the boundary where taking in more is no longer possible or safe. In this way, the Goblet helps you notice the conditions under which receiving becomes difficult, costly, or impossible, and the conditions under which something becomes possible again.

You can practice this anywhere. Sitting, standing, walking, in the middle of a conversation, in a bathroom, on a staircase, in a classroom, in a kitchen. You can practice it with eyes open. You can practice it while moving. You can practice just one part of it. You can practice it for one breath.

You are not trying to create a better state. You are only staying close to the one you are already in.

The Practice

You might begin by noticing whatever is already present. Sounds around you. Sensations in your body. The temperature of the air. The quality of your thoughts. This is the **Cup**. Nothing needs to be filtered out. Whatever is here is what is here. You are noticing what they are—perhaps sounds around you, smells, colors, textures, temperature, pressure, thoughts, images, and more. Notice them and name them. If it becomes too much, simply notice and name those that you are able to make room for.

After a moment, if it feels accessible, let the cup gently glide to the background and let your attention narrow gently toward the movement of your breath, wherever it is most noticeable right now. At the nostrils. In the chest. In the belly. Or as a general rising and falling. You can also narrow gently towards one specific anchor that feels present with a certain consistency and rhythm right now—it may be the texture of your dress, an object in your visual field, or something else. This is the **Flute**. With the breath, you are not controlling it, you are letting it be something your attention leans toward for a few moments.

Then, when you are ready, you may move the Flute to the background and feel the **Base**. This is the part of your body that is in contact with something steady. The floor beneath your feet. The chair under your body. The wall behind your back. The weight of your hands. You are not trying to feel supported. You are noticing whether support is already present in any form.

You may move between these three in any order. Or only stay with one. Or drift in and out of all of them. Even one in-breath and one out-breath is enough.

The Goblet does not remove what you are living inside. It simply allows you to touch it without having to disappear into it. Gently when you feel ready, you can move out of the practice and see if you feel moved to answer at least one of the reflection prompts. You can also go back into your day and choose not to answer these questions.

Reflection Prompts

- What did your attention move toward most easily: The first, second, or third part?
- What were you already noticing in the Cup?
- How did your body respond to narrowing attention for even a moment?
- What felt possible to receive in the Flute?
- Where did your body need support so that it didn't keep taking in more?
- Did anything soften, intensify, resist, or stay the same?
- What does this practice reveal about what you truly want, and how your current conditions shape your access to that?
- In the conditions you live in, which systems or roles require your body to stay open, available, or absorbing more than it has capacity for?

(*The last two questions do not require a perfect political analysis. You might answer it by thinking of a job, a room, a relationship, a role, or a recurring situation where your body feels it cannot afford to close, filter, or rest. It might also be a question that is answerable over time of doing the Goblet multiple times.*)

Lived Experience: Arif

Arif first began using the Goblet in moments when his body felt close to tipping over. Not in obvious crises, but in the quieter, grinding parts of the day where pressure kept accumulating without relief. At work, his role required him to absorb constant interruptions, messages arriving from multiple directions, demands layered without pause. By evening, his chest often felt tight, his jaw ached, and his thoughts raced long after he left the office.

One afternoon, after a meeting where his ideas were spoken over repeatedly, Arif stepped outside the building instead of returning directly to his desk. He did not name what he was doing as a practice. He only noticed that he could not move forward in the same way for a few minutes. Standing near the curb, he began with what was already loud in his awareness. The heat in his face. The clenching behind his eyes. The buzz of traffic, the pressure in his feet from standing too long, the irritation that kept pulsing through his chest. Nothing softened immediately. The Cup did not make him calmer. It only made the fullness visible.

After a few moments, his attention moved to the breath without effort. Not as something to steady himself, but as something that was still happening even while he felt overwhelmed. The breath was uneven. Short. A little shaky. He stayed with that without trying to fix it.

Then, gradually, his awareness dropped lower. The weight of his body through his legs. The ground beneath his shoes. The simple fact of being supported by something that was not asking anything of him. The Base did not take his stress away. It changed where the stress lived. His shoulders lowered slightly. The tightness in his jaw remained, but it no longer filled his whole field, and he allowed himself to sit on the outdoor seating by the curb to have his body feel supported more fully.

Later that evening, as Arif reflected on the moment, he realized what the practice had made visible. It was not only the pressure of the meeting. It was the cost of constantly proving his competence in spaces where he was already marked as expendable. The interruption he felt was not just professional. It was racialized. Classed. Structured by who was assumed to belong and who was expected to adapt quietly.

What shifted for Arif was not that the pressure disappeared. What shifted was that the pressure no longer collapsed entirely into self-blame. The Goblet did not regulate his nervous system into calm. It reorganized how the strain made sense in his body. In the days that followed, he noticed himself stepping away more often for brief pauses. Sometimes into the stairwell. Sometimes into the bathroom. Sometimes just into stillness at his desk. These pauses did not solve the conditions he worked within. They changed how fully those conditions could disappear into him.

For Arif, the Goblet became less about grounding and more about remembering what was being endured. Each time he felt his feet on the floor, he also felt the truth of what it was costing him to keep standing in the ways his workplace required. The practice did not make him less impacted. It made the impact harder to erase. Over time, this noticing began to shape his choices. Not all at once. Not dramatically. In small refusals. In moments of naming. In deciding when to speak and when to leave. The Goblet did not teach him to cope better. It helped him stay in relationship with what his body already knew about pressure, belonging, and the limits of what could be absorbed alone. Liberation here did not arrive as relief. It arrived as the growing impossibility of pretending that endurance was neutral.

Summary

Across this chapter, you were not asked to become more regulated, more positive, more aware, or more resilient. You were invited to notice something simpler and more fundamental: that your body is still responding. You were invited to notice, to stay, and to choose at your own pace. This is not accidental. These practices are meant to be returned to, not completed. They may be practiced alone, with others, in silence, with movement, with adaptation, with rest, or not at all on some days. They are meant to travel with you into the rest of this workbook, not as techniques to apply, but as ways of listening to how liberation already lives in the body.

Through sensing, pausing, moving, and receiving, different qualities of aliveness may have become visible. Not as achievements. Not as stable states. But as shifting capacities that come and go under changing conditions. For some, aliveness may have appeared as warmth, movement, or breath. For others, it may have appeared as irritation, heaviness, withdrawal, or the need to stop. None of these are lesser forms of life. They are honest expressions of how bodies live inside the worlds that shape them.

What shows up in the body is never only personal. Tightening in meetings, vigilance in public space, collapse after being spoken over, difficulty receiving care, or the need to keep moving are shaped inside caste hierarchies, gendered surveillance, ableist norms, psychiatric control, economic extraction, and histories of exclusion. These practices were not offered as ways to privately cope with these conditions. They were offered as ways to recognize how these conditions live in the body, and how the body has learned to respond with intelligence, protection, refusal, adaptation, and endurance. To stay with aliveness in this way is already a quiet disruption of systems that benefit from your disconnection, exhaustion, and disappearance. It does not remove those systems, but it does change how completely they can claim your body.

It is possible that some of what you noticed felt familiar. The way the breath settles when there is a small moment of relief. The way the body braces before something difficult. The way movement, repetition, touch, or stillness already help you get through the day. These are not things the practices invent. These are ways your body has already learned to live. What changes when these practices are taken up intentionally, alone or together with others, is not the presence of embodiment but the conditions around it. What is usually held alone may become shareable. What moves too quickly to be sensed may slow down. What feels unspeakable may begin to find language through the body.

Embodiment here is not something to achieve. It is something to keep returning to, as life continues to meet you in different ways.

In the next chapter, we move from simply sensing that we are alive toward exploring what becomes possible when that aliveness begins to ask for space, dignity, direction, and claim. For now, it is enough to pause here and let the body register: something in me is still responding.

How does "I Am Alive" register in your body? Draw or write your reflections in this space...

Chapter 5

Displaying What Is Our Right

Embodied Collective Action

From the time we learn to move through the world, our bodies are already responding to what is fair, what is unsafe, what must be endured, and what cannot be carried any longer. These responses are not taught through theory. They take shape through lived experience, through family, community, institutions, violence, care, belief, and survival. Long before we have language for "rights" or "justice," the body already knows when something is wrong, when a boundary has been crossed, when dignity has been interrupted, and when something inside must move outward.

In the previous chapter, "I Am Alive," you were invited into the restoration of aliveness—the sensing that the body is not only shaped by harm and pressure, but is also capable of response, rest, and movement. "Displaying What Is Our Right" grows directly from that ground. When aliveness becomes visible, the body does not only sense inwardly, there is also the orientation outward. Our bodies perhaps demonstrate an indication of what is needed and what we cannot live with. Our bodies take up space in visible ways.

This chapter does not teach you how to demand your rights. It recognizes that people already do this in countless everyday forms—through refusal, speech, silence, leaving, staying, caring, confronting, withholding, educating, protesting, and reorganizing relationships. What practice offers here is not instruction, but solidarity. It offers conditions where these responses can be noticed, reflected upon, and shaped with more care, clarity, and collective intention.

What becomes possible when bodily responses are no longer held alone?
What shifts when the longing for dignity is not hidden inside endurance?
What changes when the body's truth is witnessed in community?

"Displaying What Is Our Right" names that moment when what has been carried silently begins to take form in the world—unevenly, imperfectly, and always in relation to power, safety, privilege, and risk. The practices in this chapter are ideal to do in a small group, with one more person, or a community of people that you feel aligned with. The Pause for Perspective sangha is a space that is created for people practicing embodied social justice, you can join this space also—look up their events on Instagram. If practicing together is not felt just yet, practice in spaces where there is relative safety and comfort for reflection. It is also important to know that, like all practices, those in this current chapter are also

DOI: 10.4324/9781003672203-7

openings; there are no absolutes regarding what shows up or how you show up for the practice. Allow yourself to be led by what you feel moved or curious to engage with. While the lived experience excerpts intend to support a possibility, it may be so that they end up feeling like they are polarized and make you feel you *have to* feel a certain way. Notice how these kinds of absolutes form and bring to attention the kinds of shaping that lead us to mandates of how we need to show up. Invite another gentle perspective, if possible, in order to begin.

Practice Invitation 1: Pleasant and Unpleasant Events Record

This practice supports cultivating curiosity toward the body's daily responses to life—how it expands in connection and contracts in protest or something else. By attending to both pleasant and unpleasant experiences through the BEST (Body, Emotions, Sensations, Thoughts) framework, you see your body's intelligence as a guide toward integrity. The aim is not to label events as good or bad, but to stay close to life as it moves through you—to listen, not to fix.

You may set aside about 10 to 15 minutes each day for this practice, ideally a time when reflection and writing (if you so wish) may become possible. Keeping a notebook or journal nearby may help you record what arises. As you reflect on the week or whatever duration of time you choose to reflect on, let it be an exploration rather than a performance. Both pleasant and unpleasant moments are teachers, each carrying insight into your values and your body's natural rhythms. There is no right way to feel in this process.

Step-by-Step Practice

Each evening, settle for a few breaths and recall your day or a portion of it. Choose one pleasant and one unpleasant event that stood out. Start with the unpleasant event and once done access the pleasant event. If you were only focusing on one type of event then starting with and staying with pleasant event may be a better entry point to explore this practice and its limits. Pleasant events need not be a happy/exciting/extraordinary incident. While it can be, we are also bringing attention to everyday pleasantness, something that feels okay as well.

Write down the event first.

____

____

____

____

____

____

____

____

Next, reflect using the BEST framework. Write freely, allowing your reflections to unfold without editing or analysis.

Close each entry by asking at least one question.

- *What did I learn about myself from this experience?*
- *What action or awareness might align with my values and hopes for my community?*

You may also just let your BEST reflection be the end of this exploration.

1 *Body: What sensations did you notice—warmth, tightness, release?*

- *What did I learn about myself from this experience?*
- *What action or awareness might align with my values and hopes for my community?*

2 *Emotions: What feelings arose in that moment? How did they shift?*

- *What did I learn about myself from this experience?*
- *What action or awareness might align with my values and hopes for my community?*

3 *Sensations: What changes in breath, movement, or posture did you observe?*

- *What did I learn about myself from this experience?*
- *What action or awareness might align with my values and hopes for my community?*

4 *Thoughts: What narratives or beliefs came forward?*

- *What did I learn about myself from this experience?*
- *What action or awareness might align with my values and hopes for my community?*

Reflection Prompts

As you draw a few days' journal reflections to a close, or perhaps even one day's reflection, take some time to reflect on one of the following questions. As always, remember this is not compulsory, you can choose to skip this step.

- *What sensations tell me I am alive—in both ease and difficulty?*
- *How does my body show protest or belonging?*
- *What stories do these sensations tell about what matters to me?*
- *How can I honor both comfort and discomfort as forms of truth?*

Lived Experience: Farzana

Farzana, a queer disabled Muslim woman in her late twenties, had never tracked her days through sensations before. She expected the practice to feel abstract, almost theoretical. Instead, the process revealed itself in small, concrete ways she hadn't anticipated.

On the first evening, she sat with her notebook and thought back to a moment in her study circle. Someone had dimmed the harsh overhead light because she had mentioned her migraines earlier in the week. As she wrote about the moment, she noticed a soft warmth gathering behind her ribs. It was faint, but distinct enough to name. She wrote tentatively: *perhaps this is what "pleasant" feels like—a slight easing, nothing dramatic, but real enough to notice.*

Later in the week, an unpleasant moment surfaced when she reflected on her visit to the pharmacy. A staff member had loudly repeated instructions, assuming she could not follow them. Initially, she didn't know what to write. The memory felt too tangled. But as she sat with it, she noticed the tightness around her jaw. A familiar sensation, she wrote: *my body tightens when something feels off. I don't have the words yet, but I know this tightening means something mattered here.*

On another evening, she returned to her journal after listening to a voice note from a close friend checking in on her pain levels. This time, the pleasant moment brought tears rather than warmth. She felt startled by how quickly they came. Writing slowly, she reflected: *I didn't know care could feel overwhelming. Maybe this is also part of noticing what matters.*

By the end of the week, Farzana looked back over her entries. She didn't see big insights or fully formed interpretations. Instead, what emerged were small threads: tightness appearing in moments that felt unfair or dismissive; softness appearing when she felt considered; tears arising when care arrived unexpectedly. These patterns were subtle, but they were hers—honest, grounded, and bodily. At the bottom of the page, she wrote: *I'm not sure what all of this means yet. But I am beginning to see that my body reacts before my mind does. Maybe that's the point.* It wasn't clarity that the week offered, it was a beginning. A beginning that felt steady enough to trust, and spacious enough to return to.

Practice Invitation 2: The Five Relational Orientations of Change

These five relational orientations offer gentle ways of meeting yourself, others, and the world through the lens of impermanence, dignity, and interconnectedness. They come from the Mindfulness Based Symptom Management tradition (Five Skillful Habits) and are reimagined here through embodied social justice.

They are not rules, instructions, or expectations.
They are **doorways**—five small openings through which the body can notice how things shift, loosen, tighten, soften, and reorganize in relationship.

Impermanence shows up not only in breath and sensation but also in how we meet power, privilege, caste, race, labor, gender, ability, and desire. Systems feel rigid, yet the body shows us that change is always happening. These relational orientations help us notice that movement and respond with care, clarity, and alignment.

As you move into these relational orientations, it may help to remember that the very frameworks we use to understand care, boundaries, nourishment, or generosity are shaped by the social locations we inhabit. Caste, class, race, disability, neurodivergence, gender, and access all influence what we experience as "ethical," "healthy," or "mindful." For example, ideas about food—veganism, purity, clean eating—often arrive through caste-sanitized or class-buffered perspectives that ignore labor, affordability, or cultural belonging. This practice invites you not to judge yourself, but to notice which preferences arise from lived care and which may have been shaped by privilege or inherited narratives. This awareness allows the orientations to become spacious, relational, and just; rather than moral rules, we quietly impose on ourselves or others.

You do *not* need to explore all five. One is more than enough.

Each orientation invites a small moment of noticing, not a transformation.

These relational orientations may help you sense:

- what matters to you in the fleeting moments of daily life
- when you need to pull back or soften
- when generosity feels right-sized and when it feels forced
- what you take in from the world and how it affects your body
- how words can shape connection or distance

Taken together, these orientations remind you that Displaying What is Our Right is not a singular act but a rhythm, a movement between noticing, pausing, relating, and responding.

You may spend 10 to 30 minutes, in one sitting or spread across a day or week.

Choose a setting where you can pause without urgency: a chair, your bed, the floor, a balcony, or a quiet corner of a shared space.

Before you begin, gently ask: **Do I feel steady enough to be with even small change today?** If the answer is "not yet," you may read along without committing to a practice or come back later to practice.

Practice

Begin With Sensing

Take a few breaths.
Notice one small movement of the body, such as breath rising, warmth in your hands, weight on your feet, your heartbeat, shifting posture or such.
This is enough.

What did you notice? ____

Choose One Relational Orientation

You may explore just one, or linger with several over time. The five relational orientations are:

1 Remembering Finiteness
2 Generosity as Movement not Obligation
3 Living Boundaries
4 Nourishing Intake
5 Words as Connection

See if any of them resonate even just by reading the name and you can skip to that practice and read more about it. Alternatively, you can read all of them and decide what practice you would like to foreground. You can decide how many hours/days you would like to choose a practice and pick the others when you feel ready or curious.

1 *Remembering Finiteness*

Notice something that is ending today—daylight, a meal, a conversation, a thought you no longer feel strongly about.

Ask any one question:

- *What becomes important to me in the briefness of this moment?*
- *What makes it easier or harder for me to acknowledge endings and how might my social positioning shape my relationship to this struggle or ease of acknowledgement?*

You may begin with the smallest ending you noticed today and let your body show you what briefness reveals, without needing the answer to be clear or complete.

____
____
____
____
____

2 *Generosity as Movement, Not Obligation*

Recall a small moment when you offered or received care—something as simple as someone holding the door as they opened it before you, or a message you received, shared silence.

Ask any one question:

- *What moved in my body when connection flowed?*
- *When I offer care, is it freely given, or shaped by expectation, role, or power? Who taught me to give in this way?*

You might pause with the sensation that accompanied your giving or receiving, and gently wonder how family stories, gendered expectations, caste roles, or survival patterns shaped that movement.

3 *Living Boundaries*

Think of a moment this week when your body said, "not now," "this much," or "this is too much."

Ask any one question

- *How did my body tell me a limit was needed?*
- *Whose expectations or social norms make asserting this boundary easier or harder for me and how do privilege and marginalization shape how my "no" is received?*

You may start with the exact moment your body signaled "enough," and softly notice how your identities influence who is permitted to set limits and whose boundaries are questioned or ignored.

4 *Nourishing Intake*

Notice what you absorbed today—conversations, news, noise, silence, social media, expectations, even food.

Ask any one question:

- *What nourished me? What weighed on me? What did my body carry without choice?*
- *What do I have the privilege to turn away from or filter, and what am I required to absorb because of my identities or social location?*

As you reflect on what you took in today, you might gently notice which inputs you could choose and which were shaped by social location, labor expectations, or the demands placed on your body.

5 *Words as Connection*

Recall a conversation that stayed with you—uplifting, unsettling, confusing, grounding.

Ask any one question:

- *What did my body feel as I spoke or listened?*
- *Whose voices (including mine) are amplified or silenced in my environments, and how does my social position shape what feels safe to say?*

You may return to one moment in the conversation when your body shifted, and quietly explore how power, safety, or belonging shaped what you felt able, or unable, to voice.

____
____
____
____
____

Close Gently

Read what you have written or sensed. Underline or hold one phrase that feels alive.

End with a slow exhale and a reminder, if it is supportive, or offer to yourself another way to indicate pausing the practice.

Change is constant. Care can be too.

Consider the following reflection questions. You may choose one or more. You may skip all.

- Which relational orientation felt most approachable today, and what did my body show me as I stayed with it?
- Did anything shift in me as I noticed change (a softening, tightening, curiosity, confusion, or clarity)?
- What did I learn about what nourishes me, and what I quietly absorb that costs me something?
- Where did I sense a boundary trying to form, and what conditions might help me honor it next time?
- How did caste, race, class, gender, queerness, disability, or neurodivergence shape what felt possible to give, receive, or say today?

(*If doing this in a group, people may be invited to share only sensations or metaphors—not stories—to keep sharing safe.*)

____
____
____
____
____
____
____
____
____
____

Lived Experience: Nisha

Nisha, a 48-year-old woman with chronic pain, had been attending Pause for Perspective's Mindfulness Circle for a few months. Most weeks, she arrived straight from work, exhausted from navigating accessibility barriers that others rarely noticed—narrow office spaces, long commutes, and colleagues who expected speed she could not always offer. On this particular evening, the group was exploring the Relational Orientations of Change. When the facilitator invited everyone to choose one orientation to stay with, Nisha chose *Living Boundaries*, remembering how drained she felt after a relative had dismissed her need to rest during a family gathering. As she reflected, her breath felt tight and shallow—her body's familiar signal of being stretched beyond capacity.

As others in the circle spoke, Nisha noticed something else: some participants described "choosing boundaries" as though it was simply a matter of preference or skill. She felt a quiet awareness arise—not irritation, but clarity. For her, boundaries were not lifestyle choices. They were shaped by chronic pain, caregiving responsibilities, and gendered expectations. They were necessary for survival, not optional self-care.

A younger participant, Jay, shared how setting boundaries at work felt risky due to caste dynamics with their manager. Hearing this, Nisha felt a soft shift in her chest. She realized that while her pain limited her, she also had forms of social power—caste, class, and seniority—that shaped how her boundaries were received. She didn't feel shame, only recognition that her experience was one part of a larger landscape. Later, when she wrote in her journal, she reflected: *My boundary today wasn't just "I am tired." It was also "I am allowed to need differently." And I see that others in the circle are navigating boundaries shaped by pressures I do not face. I want to hold both truths—my limit and their realities.*

When the group closed the practice, each person shared one sentence aloud. Nisha whispered: *"May I honor what my body asks for, and may I stay awake to the freedoms and limits others live within."* For her, this was Displaying What Is Our Right—not only the right to rest and be believed, but also the right to practice awareness that was relational, political, and spacious. It did not make her pain disappear, but it softened her aloneness and widened her understanding of how bodies carry both constraint and privilege into every room.

Practice Invitation 3: Tracking What Matters

This practice invites you to notice how your body already tracks what matters—what feels right, fair, dignifying, possible, or necessary—even before you articulate it in words. Many people imagine that recognizing what we deserve must come from clarity, confidence, or certainty. Recognition of what matters may begin as a sensation—a tightening, a warmth, a pull toward something, a recoil against something else.

Displaying What Is Our Right is not about demanding or performing worthiness. It begins with noticing the quiet places where the body already says this matters, this can no longer be absorbed, or this is the world I long for. Tracking What Matters helps surface these signals so they are not swallowed by habit, politeness, fear, urgency, or inherited roles.

It does not ask you to decide anything.
It only asks you to notice what the body already knows.

You may take 5–10 minutes for this practice in any posture that feels supportive enough—sitting, standing, reclining, or moving gently, with eyes open or closed. You can pause or stop at any moment. Before beginning, remind yourself that there is no requirement to become certain or to justify what arises. You are not looking for clarity or answers. You are simply noticing where your body leans, recoils, softens, tightens, reaches, or waits. This noticing is enough.

Before you begin, you may hold a few gentle invitations with you: what matters to you is not a performance, it is a response shaped by your life and its conditions; confusion, numbness, hesitation, or even silence are also forms of response. You are allowed to notice without needing to act, decide, or arrive at clarity yet.

The Practice

When you feel ready, you may gently place the question in the room with you: *What do I want?*

You are not looking for a correct answer.
You are not searching for a single truth.
You are simply letting the question land in your body.

You might notice where the question goes first.
Does it land in the chest?
In the throat?
In the belly?
Does it scatter?
Does it go quiet?

Where does the question land for me? ____

There is no need to chase it. Allow all answers, even what you may think of "most silly" or "preposterous" as welcome, allowing all answers to sit on the shelf without preference over one or the other just yet.

Write your answers in this space...

After a few moments, you may ask again, a little slower: *What do I want, in the place where my life meets the lives of others?*

You might pause after asking, letting the body respond in its own time.
A sensation may arise.
A memory.
A longing.
A resistance.
A blankness.
All are part of the field of wanting.

If the question feels too large, you may soften it:

What matters to me right now?
What do I need more space for?
What do I wish were possible for my community?

You may notice what shifts when the question expands beyond the individual self and touches the places where your life interweaves with caste, race, class, gender, queerness, disability, labor, and the worlds you move through.

There is no urgency here.

You might stay with whatever arises as sensation—a warmth, a tightening, a pull forward, a slight withdrawal—even if no words come.

Write your answers in this space...

And when you feel ready, you may expand the inquiry: *What do I really want* —
when I listen from the part of me that refuses harm,
that longs for dignity,
that remembers solidarity,
that knows I deserve to live in a world shaped by justice?

Write your answers in this space...

You do not need to write anything down unless it feels supportive.
You may speak aloud, whisper, draw, or simply breathe with the question.

The practice ends not with an answer, but with the awareness that wanting, even quietly, even uncertainly, is itself a form of aliveness and a way of displaying what is your right.

Post-Practice Reflection Questions

You may choose one or multiple questions, or you may decide to skip this process entirely. These questions can be explored in groups also. Choose one, perhaps, that you feel most drawn to share.

- What did I notice in my body as I sat with the question "What do I want?"
- How did my body respond when the question widened from "What do we want?" or "What do I want in relation with others?"
- What pressures, expectations, or inherited rules shaped what felt possible—or not possible—to want?
- What small action, pause, boundary, or conversation might honor what surfaced for me and for the communities I belong to?

Lived Experience: Farah

Farah joined a weekly group at her community center, mostly for the company. The practice *What do I want?* felt abstract to her, almost unrealistic. Most days she was focused on simply getting through work, managing home responsibilities, and navigating the unspoken tensions in her extended family. During the session, when the facilitator invited everyone to settle and let the question land in their bodies, Farah felt an unexpected tightening along her jaw. Not a thought—a sensation. As if something in her was holding itself still.

When the question widened to *What do I want in the places where my life meets the lives of others?*, a pressure gathered behind Farah's eyes. A memory surfaced: sitting in a family prayer gathering where a relative joked that "queer people are just confused," and the room chuckled while she kept her gaze on the floor. Another moment followed. A work meeting where she hesitated to ask for captions during a fast-paced presentation because she didn't want to be seen as "too demanding." Her body remembered the effort of shrinking these parts of herself: the tightening in her throat, the way her shoulders rounded inward to avoid attention. As she stayed with the sensations, a quiet truth emerged. Her longing was not for perfection or acceptance from everyone. It was for spaces where her queer, Muslim, disabled body did not have to fragment itself to belong—where she could move, speak, and ask for what she needed without anticipating harm. The wanting felt small and unmistakably alive: *I want rooms where I can remain whole.*

In the group room, she did not share any of this out loud. She simply noticed her breath becoming shallow and her hands curling slightly on her lap. Another participant mentioned feeling pressure in their ribs when the question touched on community. Someone else said they realized they wanted more safety at home. The facilitator kept reminding the group: *You are only noticing, not deciding.* When it was Farah's turn to speak, she didn't relay the incidents or the politics. Instead, she placed two fingers lightly on her throat and said, "*I noticed something tight here. Like a word that keeps stopping before it comes out.*" The group nodded softly, recognizing the kind of silence she was pointing to without needing the details.

On her walk home, Farah felt a quieter, more grounded knowing in her chest: *I want space to speak when something is untrue or unjust.* Not to confront everything, not to become forceful or perfect, but to stop leaving herself behind in rooms where harm slips by unnoticed. Nothing resolved that evening. No decisions were made. But for the first time, Farah recognized that wanting a different way of showing up—for herself, and alongside others harmed by casteism, by gender norms, by erasure—was itself a movement of Displaying What Is Our Right.

The wanting had shape now. It had context. It had a pulse.

And the group had offered her enough safety to feel it.

Practice Invitation 4: Declarations of Commitment

As an extension to the previous practice, Declarations of Commitment invite you to listen for the directions your body already leans toward, rather than setting goals to be achieved. This version honors that in trauma and oppression the body has often been trained to brace, comply, or overperform. Here, you are invited to declare—not by force, but by attunement—what you care about and how you want to relate to your commitments with kindness.

Declarations become living intentions that you return to again and again, like a small candle you tend, not a torch you must carry.

You may take about 20–40 minutes for this practice, moving slowly or returning to it in parts if that feels more supportive.

Choose any setting where you can pause, reflect, and rest. This might be a quiet room, your bed, a balcony, or even a parked vehicle. You might keep soft music, a comforting scent, a warm cup of tea, or an object that symbolizes safety nearby.

Before beginning, check in with your body and ask, "*Do I have the capacity to explore this now?*" If the answer feels uncertain, you may begin with other practices, such as the Goblet or the Body Scan, and return to this practice at another time. Like the previous practice you may choose to partake in a group where you can do it together.

Begin with Listening

Take a few slow breaths and gently ask your body, "*What matters to me right now?*"

You can use one or more sentences that came from your previous practice exploration, or you might explore one of the following questions:

- What or who do I care about deeply?
- What do I long to nurture or protect?
- Who am I becoming when I am most connected to life?

____

____

____

____

____

If answers feel fuzzy, notice any sensations that arise with tightness, warmth, tears, or quiet. Let the body speak before words do.

Phrase Your Declaration as an Invitation

Rather than a definitive statement, try framing your declaration as an unfolding relationship:

- *I am tending to…*
- *I am exploring how to…*
- *I am in practice with…*
- *I am remembering my wish to…*

Examples:

- *I am tending to presence and honesty in my relationships.*
- *I am remembering my wish to rest when I am tired.*
- *I am in practice with creating space for collective care.*

Speak each phrase aloud. See where it lands in your body—soft, uncertain, steady. All are welcome.

Identify Conditions of Support

Ask:

- *What helps me stay connected to this intention?*
- *Who or what helps me remember it when I forget?*
- *What do I need to feel safe enough to keep practicing?*

Write down sensory reminders—warm tea, a walk outside, a supportive friend—anything that signals return rather than pressure.

Move Toward Gentle Action

If the body feels ready, name one small next step: a conversation, a pause, a creative act, a boundary, or rest. Let the step be sized to your current capacity. *Micro-actions* are legitimate movements of liberation.

Engage in Relational Witnessing

Invite someone you trust to listen as you share your declaration. You might ask them not for feedback, but for reflection:

- *What do you hear in my words that feels alive?*
- *What feels steady or tender in how I say this?*

Allow their witnessing to deepen your sense of connection and belonging.

Reflection Prompts

See if you feel moved to reflect on this practice with one question. You may skip this reflection or come back to it later if you so wish.

- What felt alive or steady as I shaped my declaration?
- Where in my body did I notice ease or resistance?
- What helps me stay connected to this intention when I lose sight of it?
- How can I honor that my commitment, like my body, changes and adapts over time?

Lived Experience: Leela

Leela sat in the group circle with her notebook open but untouched, waiting for her body to settle. As a queer woman from a mixed-caste background working in disability advocacy, she was used to carrying multiple layers of vigilance into any room. Her shoulders stayed slightly lifted, as if preparing for correction or misunderstanding even before a word was spoken. When the facilitator invited the group into the practice of Declarations, Leela felt the familiar tightness in her throat—a body-memory from years of being told to soften her tone, to be grateful, to adjust herself to fit into caste-coded, productivity-driven professional spaces. But she also felt something else: the steady presence of the group, neurodivergent and neurotypical, queer and trans, disabled and non-disabled, across religions and caste marginalization. Their quiet breathing created a kind of collective permission she wasn't used to.

When she asked herself, *What matters to me right now?* a memory rose immediately—a team meeting earlier that week where she had been interrupted multiple times. Her chest tightened recalling it, but then another memory surfaced right behind it: a moment last month when she herself had hesitated to affirm a trans colleague's pronouns because she feared "making a mistake." The realization hit with a warmth in her cheeks—not shame, but recognition.

My rights and my blind spots live side by side in my body.

The question deepened: *What do I want, in the place where my life meets the lives of others?*

Her breath shifted, softer now. She wrote:

May I speak from my truth without shrinking.
May I make room for truths that are not shaped like mine.
May I honor the rights I need and the rights I have struggled to recognize in others.
May we build spaces where access, pronouns, pace, and difference are not negotiations but conditions of belonging.

When the group was invited to speak their declarations aloud, Leela felt her voice tremble but stayed present. As she said the words, she noticed her palms warming, a sensation she often felt when something *real* came forward.

Later that evening, at home, she returned to her declaration. She wrote:

- *When my trans colleague shared their exhaustion last week, I only nodded. I didn't ask what support they needed. My silence wasn't neutrality; it was fear of doing it wrong.*
- *I want to practice seeing where my comfort becomes someone else's isolation.*

Her chest softened as she wrote. She realized that Displaying What Is Our Right also meant disrupting the idea that only *some* rights mattered in the room.

Two days later, she met her accountability partner— Aarav, a neurodivergent organizer. She read her declaration aloud. He listened quietly and said, "*What I hear is that your dignity and their dignity are not two separate practices for you. They're one movement.*" His words landed in her belly—grounding, steady. The next week, when a colleague used the wrong pronouns for someone in their team, Leela felt the familiar tightening in her throat but this time, it loosened into clarity. She gently said, "*They use they/them*," her tone warm, not corrective. Her body felt aligned, not with performance but with practice. The declaration had not made her confident. It had made her *willing*.

And willingness, she realized, was its own form of aliveness.

Practice Invitation 5: Coming Up with Phrases of Compassionate Assertion

This practice supports you in embodying Displaying What Is Our Right, the outward expression of liberation through intentional, compassionate assertion. While aliveness begins within, the movement toward justice unfolds when the body's knowing is voiced and shared.

Rooted in compassion, this practice helps you identify and articulate personal and collective rights that matter to you. The intention is not to create slogans of resistance alone, but to form embodied invitations—words that arise from your lived truth, carried by awareness and care.

The hope of this practice is to transform felt knowing into areas of influence. You learn to name, embody, and declare what is already your right, while remaining attentive to systemic realities and relational safety. Compassionate Assertion becomes the bridge between inner conviction and collective voice—grounded, kind, and powerfully clear.

You may take 15–25 minutes for this practice whenever you feel steadiness or curiosity. Choose a place where you can settle a little, write, or simply sit with your thoughts. Before you begin, pause for a few breaths and check in with your body—just enough to sense whether you feel supported enough to explore what is true for you today. If the body feels unsure or overwhelmed, you can return to a simpler practice in this chapter, or earlier ones, or come back to this reflection later, perhaps with someone who can gently witness your process.

As you enter the practice, you might hold in mind that these phrases are not demands of yourself. They are expressions of dignity and care. Compassion can soften the edges as you reflect, helping your voice find its own pace and shape. Your words do not need to be final or polished. They can shift and change over time. This practice is something you can grow into rather than get right.

Step-by-Step Practice Reflect on What Matters

Settle into a comfortable posture. Take three slow breaths. Ask yourself: *What personal right or quality do I most need to claim or tend to right now?*

Examples: the right to rest, to express grief, to speak truth, to create without fear.

Write any phrases that arise. You can use phrases from previous practice too.

Next, ask: *What collective right or value do I long to see upheld in my community?*

Examples: shared safety, collective care, honest dialogue, belonging for all bodies.

Write freely, noticing any sensations—tightness, warmth, fluttering—that signal what feels alive or urgent.

Formulate Your "May I…" and "May We…" Phrases

Transform your reflections into compassionate assertions, beginning with *May I…* and *May we…*

- *May I practice resting when I'm tired.*
- *May I speak my truth without fear of dismissal.*
- *May we create spaces where neurodivergent voices are heard.*
- *May we hold each other in dignity and care.*

Craft 3–4 phrases that feel like genuine, embodied wishes. Let them be invitations rather than commands.

Embody and Crystalize

When you feel ready, you may let your body hold the words you have shaped. You can sit or stand—whatever posture feels steady enough. If it helps, place a hand on your heart as you speak your *May I…* phrases, and a hand on your belly or your side body as you speak your *May we…* phrases, letting the body feel the difference between the two.

Read each phrase aloud on an exhale, slowly enough that you can sense how it lands. Notice any shifts—a softening, a tightening, a quietening, a small tremble in the voice, or a settling of the breath. These are all part of how the body recognizes what is true for you. If a phrase feels sharp, heavy, or distant, you may adjust it until it feels more honest, more kind, or more possible. This is not a performance. It is a conversation with your own dignity.

If you are practicing in a group, you may gather all the phrases into a bowl or simply into a shared space. One person can read them aloud for the group to hear. Let the words fall around you like offerings; some may land gently, some may stir something awake, some may feel unfamiliar but compelling. You might notice a phrase from someone else that feels like it belongs to you too, or a phrase of yours that seems to resonate for others. This shared listening can deepen the sense that your personal declarations live within a larger collective longing.

There is no need to arrive anywhere. Let the practice end when your body feels complete—even if the declarations feel unfinished. They are meant to evolve with you.

Reflection Prompts

- Which phrases felt most alive in my body?
- What sensations signaled alignment or resistance?
- How do these phrases reflect both my individuality and my community?
- Where might I begin to live these words, even in small ways, today?

Lived Experience: Lata and Sam

Lata, a 32-year-old autistic woman with chronic pain, had been attending the weekly practice group with her partner Sam, who is neurotypical. Their relationship was loving, but their sensory worlds were different in ways neither of them had learned to name. Sam preferred spontaneous plans, long conversations, background music always playing. Lata needed predictability, quiet transitions, and less sensory input—needs she often suppressed to "keep the peace," especially because Sam did not intentionally cause harm. She simply didn't want to be seen as overly sensitive or difficult.

During the Declarations of Commitment session, the group sat scattered on cushions and chairs. When the facilitator invited the inward question, *What matters to me right now?*, Lata felt a small ache gather behind her eyes. Her first sensation wasn't clarity. It was fatigue. The kind that arrives when masking has gone on too long. She softened the question: *What do I need more space for, in myself and in this relationship?*

Her body answered before words did: a tightness in her jaw, a subtle recoil at the thought of another weekend of back-to-back social plans. She wrote her first phrase slowly:

"*May I name my limits without feeling like a burden.*"

Then, when the prompt widened to collective longing, she surprised herself by writing:

"*May we create a rhythm that honors both our nervous systems.*"

These words felt real—not aspirational, not performative, but lived.

When the group placed their declarations into the communal bowl and read them aloud, Sam heard Lata's phrases before knowing they were hers. Something in Sam's face softened. Later, during partner reflection rounds, Sam quietly said, "*I didn't know it weighed on you like that. I want to understand.*"

Back at home that night, Lata shared a concrete example she had never said aloud: when Sam played music while cooking, the overlapping sensations—the sizzling, the beat, their conversation—overloaded her senses. She loved being with Sam in the kitchen but often left abruptly because her body simply couldn't take it. She had assumed Sam would view this as rejection or rigidity. Sam listened, not defensively but attentively. "*If music off makes it easier for you to stay with me,*" they said, "*I can do that. I didn't know.*" It wasn't a grand moment of transformation, just a small shift in recognition, but it loosened something inside Lata, a long-held belief that her needs were "too much." She felt her breath deepen, as if the body were saying, *this is a right, not a favor.*

Two days later, Lata messaged her accountability partner from the group: "*I finally named what I need. It wasn't dramatic. It was gentle. And it felt like claiming something that had always belonged to me.*" For Lata, Displaying What Is Our Right was not about assertiveness in a heroic sense. It was the quiet, relational practice of letting her truth be seen without shrinking it to protect others and without demanding that others change overnight.

Her declaration lived on her bedside table: "*May I trust that my needs do not diminish connection; they deepen it.*"

And for the first time, she believed it enough to practice it—one small moment at a time.

Summary

Displaying What Is Our Right is not a single act, nor a moment of certainty. It is a slow, relational unfolding in which the body remembers itself in the world and the world is asked, even quietly, to make room for that remembering. Across this chapter, you have practiced noticing what matters, naming longings shaped by your life and its conditions, articulating declarations that arise from truth rather than pressure, and exploring how care, boundaries, generosity, speech, and change live in your daily movements. These practices do not create dignity; they help you recognize where dignity already lives in you, and how it becomes visible through small gestures, refusals, pauses, invitations, and collective longings.

Displaying your right takes many forms. In movements and communities it can be loud, unified, and reverberating—a force that propels change, confronts injustice, and reshapes collective life. And in the beginnings of practice, in the intimacy of daily living, it often arrives more quietly. It shows itself in subtle, relational, bodily shifts: a breath that deepens, a boundary spoken gently, a pause that interrupts urgency, a longing named aloud for the first time, a refusal to shrink or overperform. These quieter movements are not less powerful; they are the ground from which louder collective expressions can eventually grow.

As you move through your own life, you may find that your right to belonging, rest, safety, truth, and connection is expressed not only through words but also through breath, posture, choice, silence, and the ways you orient toward others. Displaying your right is shaped by caste, race, class, queerness, disability, neurodivergence, gender, and the landscapes you move through—and it remains adaptable, responsive, and alive.

You do not have to hold these movements alone. Your declarations can be witnessed by those who walk beside you; your longings can be shared with people and spaces that honor your becoming. Over time, what you name, tend to, and express becomes part of a wider collective rhythm. Displaying What Is Our Right is both personal and communal—a way of aligning your body with the world you want to help build, breath by breath, choice by choice.

You may return to any practice in this chapter whenever you wish. Each one meets you where you are, and each one trusts that your body already carries the wisdom it needs. The work is simply to listen, to pause, and to allow what is dynamic to take shape.

How does "*Displaying What Is Our Right*" align your body with the world you want to co-create? Draw or write your reflections in this space...

Part III

Body as a Site of Protest

The earlier chapters attended to moments of aliveness, expansion, display, and the claiming of one's right to exist and take up space. These moments were shaped by conditions where the body could lean toward expression, choice, and movement, even when that movement was careful or uneven.

This section begins from a different bodily location.

Body as a Site of Protest centers bodies for whom expansion is not always possible, safe, or strategic. It centers bodies whose relationship to the world is shaped by constraint rather than choice, and by survival rather than visibility. These are bodies navigating caste or race violence, gendered surveillance, ableism, queerphobia, Islamophobia, class precarity, neurodivergent exclusion, and their intersections. For these bodies, a typical understanding of 'moving forward' is not always liberatory. Speaking is not always protective. Being seen is not always an option.

Here, the body does not reach outward.
It withholds.

Protest, in this frame, does not announce itself through action or declaration. It often appears quietly, through slowing down, going still, withdrawing attention, becoming silent, or shutting parts of oneself away. These responses are frequently misunderstood as passivity, disengagement, or personal limitation. In this work, they are understood as something else entirely.

They are embodied refusals shaped by lived knowledge of consequence.

When systems demand participation without safety, explanation without care, or endurance without dignity, the body may refuse. That refusal is not the absence of response. It is a response formed through experience. In embodied social justice, protest is not measured by how visible it is. It is measured by what it is protecting.

This section invites you to meet protest at this quieter register. It asks what becomes possible when we stop asking the body to move toward liberation and, instead, listen to what it is refusing to carry.

DOI: 10.4324/9781003672203-8

As you prepare to explore '*Body as a Site of Protest*', what is happening in your body at this time? Draw or write your reflections in this space...

Chapter 6

Freeze as Protest

Recognizing Bodily Shutdown

Not all bodies can move toward liberation in the same ways or at the same pace. For some, reaching outward brings relief or possibility. For others, it brings scrutiny, punishment, or loss. Over time, the body learns which forms of engagement are survivable and which are not. When expression has been met with harm, protest often turns inward. It settles into posture, breath, sensation, and absence. The body becomes precise about where it cannot go.

Freeze emerges here.

Freeze: Refusal to Engage

Freeze names one of the ways protest lives in the body when engagement itself becomes unsafe. In this chapter, refusal does not take the form of action, voice, or visibility. It takes the form of withholding. For many marginalized bodies, participation carries cost. Speaking may invite punishment. Explaining may invite erasure. Moving forward may require abandoning parts of oneself in order to remain intact. Freeze emerges in these conditions, not as a failure to cope, but as a bodily assessment of risk.

Freeze is not the opposite of liberation. It is not a step backward. It is what happens when the conditions required for liberation are not present. It reflects the body's recognition that engagement would come at too great a cost.

Freeze is not a stage to move through. It is not a precursor to confidence, clarity, or power. It is a complete response shaped by survival. Silence, numbness, stillness, withdrawal, and shutdown are understood here as intentional refusals, even when they are not chosen consciously.

The practices in this chapter of the workbook do not aim to soften Freeze or prepare the body for re-engagement. They are offered as ways of recognizing Freeze as protest, and of staying with it without pressure to change, explain, or overcome it.

Conditions That Support This Work

Freeze does not emerge in isolation. It is shaped by repeated encounters with risk, erasure, punishment, and loss of access. Because of this experience, the conditions under which Freeze is approached matter as much as the practices themselves. Without care towards

DOI: 10.4324/9781003672203-9

these conditions, even well-intentioned practices can reproduce the very dynamics that taught the body to withdraw in the first place.

This work begins with permission.

You are not required to complete this chapter to move on to the next. You are not required to engage with every practice. You are not required to explain what arises for you, either to yourself or to others. Choosing not to participate, stopping midway, or returning later are not forms of avoidance. Here, in this space, they are expressions of discernment. Freeze has already learned how to protect you. The practices offered in this section of the workbook do not ask your body to unlearn that skill.

Pacing is central to the journey in this chapter. These practices are not meant to be done quickly, nor are they meant to create insight on demand. If a practice feels distant, irritating, or inaccessible, that response is meaningful. It may be signaling that the conditions for this work are not present right now. Listening to that signal is part of the practice.

Safety, in the context of Freeze, is not a feeling state. It is a structural condition. Where and with whom this work is done shapes what becomes possible. Safety is not determined by whether a group is mixed-identity or homogeneous, but by whether the specific site of protest being worked with is shared, named, and protected. Freeze emerges in response to particular systems of harm. A body that freezes around caste exclusion may not feel safe working with that Freeze in a group where caste is unnamed or minimized. A body that freezes around queer visibility may not feel safe in a space where queerness is treated as abstract identity rather than lived risk.

Groups can support Freeze work when there is clarity about what is being protested, and when participants understand whether they are inside that protest or witnessing it. This clarity matters because Freeze often deepens when explanation is expected. When silence is treated as something that needs to be filled, or when stillness is interpreted as disengagement, the body learns again that withdrawal is necessary.

In the early stages of Freeze work, many people find it safer to practice with a trusted mental health professional while also experimenting with these practices on their own. Solitude can reduce the pressure to perform, narrate, or reassure others. Practicing on one's own does not mean practicing without support. It means allowing the body to sense without being watched.

When Freeze work is done in groups, certain conditions help reduce harm. These include explicit permission to remain silent, the absence of pressure to share personal stories, and an understanding that participation may look like stillness, distance, or minimal engagement. Groups that prioritize learning, dialogue, or collective processing too early can unintentionally override the protective function of Freeze. It is also important to name that not all groups are appropriate spaces for this work. Spaces where power differences are active and unnamed, such as workplaces, classrooms, or mixed settings where marginalized experiences are routinely questioned or explained away, may not be safe places to explore Freeze. Choosing not to bring this work into such spaces is not a limitation. It is an act of care.

Before moving into any practice in this chapter, you may want to pause and ask yourself quietly what would help your body feel less exposed right now. The answer may be to practice alone, to choose a practice that involves minimal inward focus, or to skip the practice altogether. That choice is not separate from the work. It is the work.

What comes to mind as you ask your body, "*What would help you feel less exposed right now?*" Draw or write your responses in this space…

This chapter does not aim to make Freeze go away. It aims to create conditions where Freeze does not have to work so hard to protect you.

Practice Invitation 1: Anchored Sensory Grounding with Systemic Awareness

This practice is offered as a way of staying oriented without asking the body to open, resolve, or explain itself. It is especially relevant for moments when the body has withdrawn, gone quiet, or feels distant, and when engagement with the world has become effortful or unsafe. Rather than trying to bring the body back into participation, this practice allows the body to remain where it is, while offering a point of contact that does not demand change.

Anchoring here is not about calming down or stabilizing the nervous system. It is about having something to lean on while freeze is present. The anchor serves as a steady reference point, allowing the body's refusal to exist without being interrogated.

Before beginning, it may help to choose a time when you are not already overwhelmed. You might be sitting, lying down, standing, or gently moving. There is no correct posture. If focusing on bodily sensation feels intrusive or activating, you can remain oriented to the external world throughout the practice. Sound, light, texture, or temperature are all valid anchors. You are free to open your eyes, move, or stop at any moment.

As you begin, allow yourself to arrive without expectation. There is nothing to settle into and nothing to accomplish. You might simply notice that you are here, in this moment, with whatever your body is carrying. If even that feels like too much, let your attention rest outside of you, perhaps on a sound in the room or the feeling of a surface supporting you.

When you are ready, choose one anchor that feels most accessible right now. This could be the hum of a fan, the weight of your body against a chair, the coolness of the floor beneath your feet, or the sight of something steady in your environment.

My chosen anchor is: ____

Let your attention rest there lightly. It does not need to stay fixed. Drifting and returning are both part of the practice. As you remain with the anchor, you may become aware of other sensations in your body. There may be areas that feel tight, numb, heavy, distant, or difficult to sense at all. There is no need to move toward these sensations or to understand them. If they come into awareness, allow them to be there without commentary. You might quietly acknowledge, *something in me is holding back*, or *something in me is protecting me right now.*

If at any point emotion, discomfort, or dissociation intensifies, return fully to your anchor. You might open your eyes, shift your position, or end the practice altogether. Ending early is not interruption. It is completion.

When you are ready to finish, allow your attention to widen again. Notice the space around you, the quality of light, the sounds present. There is no closing ritual required. You are simply leaving the practice in the way that best supports you.

Reflections

(Answer one or more question, or skip altogether)

- What anchor felt most accessible to you in this moment?
- What did your body seem to be protecting you from, if anything?
- What was it like to let sensations remain without trying to change them?
- How did it feel to stay with your body without asking it to explain or move?

____

____

____

____

____

____

____

____

____

____

____

Lived Experience: Meher

Meher is part of a small project team that meets online every week. The meetings move quickly, with people speaking over one another and shifting topics without pause. Meher usually keeps her camera on and contributes when she can, but in recent weeks she has noticed herself growing quieter. During one meeting, she feels her throat tighten as a colleague repeats an idea Meher had shared earlier, this time receiving immediate affirmation. Meher considers speaking up, then decides against it. Her body feels heavy, as though it has settled deeper into the chair.

After the meeting ends, Meher does not immediately return to her work. She swivels slightly in her chair and places one hand flat on the desk in front of her. The surface feels cool and solid beneath her palm. She notices the faint buzzing sound of the ceiling fan above her. Her breath feels uneven, shallow in places, but she does not try to adjust it. For several minutes, she stays like this, hand on the desk, listening to the fan. Her shoulders remain raised. There is still a tightness in her throat. She notices an urge to replay the meeting in her mind, to think of what she could have said differently. She lets her attention return to the sound, over and over.

At one point, a thought arises: *I should say something next time.* It stays present as she moves to listen to the buzzing of the ceiling fan. What remains is a quiet recognition that her silence was not confusion or lack of clarity. It was her body declining further exposure in a space where being heard felt uncertain.

When Meher eventually turns back to her screen, the tightness has not disappeared. The meeting has not been resolved. But there is a sense of having stayed with herself, rather than pushing past what her body had already decided.

Practice Invitation 2: Unpleasant Event Record as Protest (BEST)

This practice invites you to stay with an unpleasant or constraining moment from your day, and approach it as an instance of protest rather than a personal difficulty. It is grounded in the understanding that many everyday moments of discomfort arise not because something is wrong with us, but because our bodies are responding to expectations that erase, diminish, or overextend us.

In the context of Freeze, unpleasant experiences often carry subtle bodily signals of refusal. These signals may appear as tension, heaviness, numbness, irritation, withdrawal, or fatigue. This practice does not ask you to work through the event or to arrive at clarity. It asks you to witness how your body responded, and to consider that response as meaningful in itself.

Before beginning, choose a time in your day when you feel resourced enough to briefly reflect. It may be in the morning after your first cup of coffee, or at the end of the day before you head to bed. This practice does not require revisiting traumatic events. Ordinary moments are often more revealing. If recalling an event feels activating, you are welcome to stay oriented to the present by noticing sound, temperature, or touch, and to return to the reflection only if it feels possible.

You may write, speak aloud, draw, or think quietly. There is no preferred form. Keep the reflection short. Five to ten minutes is sufficient.

Begin by bringing to mind one moment from your day that felt unpleasant, constraining, or slightly off. It may be something small: being interrupted, feeling overlooked, receiving a message at the wrong time, noticing an expectation you could not meet. Let the memory remain lightly held, without entering into detail.

Briefly write about the moment in this space...

As you stay with this moment, gently notice how your body remembers it. You might sense tightness, a dullness, a heaviness, or a pulling away. You may also notice very little. Whatever is present is enough.

You can then move through the experience using the BEST frame, not as an analysis but as a way of listening.

Notice the Body first. Where do you sense this experience now? Is there a particular place that feels activated, quiet, or absent?

Then *attend to Emotions, if any are present*. You do not need to name them precisely. It may be enough to sense that something emotional is here, or that emotion feels distant.

Next, *notice Sensations*. This might include changes in breath, posture, temperature, or energy. Even small shifts count.

Finally, *notice Thoughts*. These may include judgments, expectations, or internalized rules such as "I should handle this better" or "This is not worth reacting to."

After moving through these layers, allow yourself to ask one gentle question: *How might my body's response be a refusal to be erased, rushed, or diminished in this moment?*

You are not looking for a definitive answer. You are simply allowing the possibility that the body's discomfort or withdrawal was protecting something important.

When you are ready to end the practice, return to a present-moment anchor. You might notice your feet on the floor, the surface supporting you, or a sound in the room. Let the reflection close without conclusion.

Reflective Questions

You may wish to deepen your practice by taking some time to reflect on one or more of the following questions:

- What bodily sensations were most noticeable as you recalled the event?
- What expectations or internal rules showed up in your thoughts?
- In what way might your body's response have been protecting you?
- How does it feel to consider this moment as protest rather than personal difficulty?

Lived Experience: Natasha

Natasha notices she has a gap between meetings in the afternoon and decides to sit on the couch for a few minutes. Earlier that day, she had received a message from her partner expressing affection and appreciation. On the surface, the message was warm and reassuring. As she read it, however, Natasha felt an immediate tightening in her jaw and shoulders. She replied politely, then put her phone down.

Later, as she begins the Unpleasant Event Record as Protest (BEST) practice, Natasha brings that moment to mind. She does not reread the message. She simply remembers the sensation of her body stiffening. As she sits, she notices the tension again, particularly along her shoulders and at the base of her neck. Her jaw feels clenched. She names this quietly as the body remembering.

Emotion is less clear. There is a faint irritation, but also something heavier beneath it. She does not try to sort it out.

As she stays with the sensations, she notices her breath feels held, as though she is bracing. A thought passes through her mind: *I should be able to receive care*. Another follows quickly: *Why am I making this difficult?* Natasha pauses here and asks herself how her body's response might be a refusal. Almost immediately, she remembers that the previous evening's conflict with her partner had ended without resolution. The affection, arriving without acknowledgment of that rupture, had felt like a request to move on before she was ready.

Her body, she realizes, had not rejected the relationship or the care. It had refused to bypass what still needed attention.

This recognition does not soften the tension right away. But something settles. Natasha sends a brief message later that evening, naming that she wants to return to the earlier conversation before continuing as usual. When she puts the phone down again, her shoulders are still tight, but the tension now feels intelligible rather than confusing.

She does not linger with this insight. She stands up, stretches lightly, and moves on with her day.

Practice Invitation 3: Withholding Engagement—Staying Without Responding

This practice invites you to notice moments when your body chooses not to engage, even in small ways. These moments often occur when a response is expected, when participation is assumed, or when silence is subtly discouraged. In many settings, not responding is read as avoidance, rudeness, or lack of interest. In this practice, it is approached as intentional non-participation, shaped by the body's assessment of risk and cost.

Withholding engagement does not mean withdrawing completely from a situation. It may look like staying present while choosing not to speak, not explain, not reassure, or not offer emotional labor. For bodies that have learned that engagement often leads to harm, this withholding can be a precise and protective form of protest.

Before beginning, it may help to choose a recent or recurring situation where you noticed yourself pulling back. This could be a conversation, a meeting, a family interaction, or an online exchange. You do not need to revisit the event in detail. The focus here is on how your body chose not to engage.

Name the situation: ____

As you bring this situation to mind, notice what happens in your body when you imagine yourself *not responding*. You may sense stillness, heaviness, relief, tension, or nothing at all. There is no need to evaluate these sensations. Simply let them be present.

Use this space to note down what happens in your body.

Rather than asking why you did not respond, see if you can stay with the experience of not doing. Not answering the question. Not clarifying your position. Not smoothing things over. Notice what it is like to remain in that space without moving toward action or explanation.

If judgment arises, either from within or from imagined others, notice how your body reacts to that pressure. Does it brace, go quiet, harden, or retreat further? These responses are part of the practice. They offer information about what engagement would have required from you.

You may remain with this noticing for a few moments, or longer, if it feels supportive. When you are ready to end the practice, orient again to your surroundings. There is no closure needed beyond acknowledging that your body made a choice.

Reflections

(*You may respond to any one question, more than one, or none at all.*)

- What did you notice in your body when you stayed without responding?
- What pressures to engage or explain became visible through this practice?
- In what ways might withholding engagement be protective rather than avoidant?
- What would it cost your body to respond in that situation?

____

____

____

____

____

____

____

____

____

____

Lived Experience: Aarav

Aarav works in a team where meetings are framed as collaborative, but decisions are often already made. During one meeting, a senior colleague asks for "any thoughts" on a plan that Aarav knows will increase workload without additional support. Aarav feels a familiar tightening in his chest. He considers speaking, then feels his energy drop.

Instead of pushing himself to respond, Aarav stays quiet. He keeps his camera on. He listens. His body feels heavy, but also strangely steady. After the meeting, he notices a wave of guilt, followed by irritation. He tells himself he should have said something.

Later, as he reflects on this practice, Aarav notices that his silence was not confusion. It was recognition. Speaking would have required him to argue for something he already knew would not be taken seriously. His body had opted out of a performance that would have cost him more than it offered. The silence did not change the outcome of the meeting. But it protected him from another round of self-doubt and depletion. In that sense, it was not absence. It was refusal.

Practice Invitation 4: Staying with the No—Not Moving, Not Explaining

This practice is for moments when the body has already said no, and there is pressure—internal or external—to move past that refusal. Often, Freeze is followed by a secondary demand: to understand it, to justify it, to soften it, or to turn it into something actionable. This practice interrupts that demand. It invites you to stay with the body's *no* without translating it into insight, intention, or next steps.

Before beginning, choose a moment when you do not need to be anywhere else immediately. This is not a practice to fit into a gap. It is a practice of not moving on.

You may sit, lie down, or remain exactly as you are. There is no instruction to settle, ground, or become present. If you notice the urge to adjust your posture, deepen your breath, or "do the practice correctly," see if you can notice that urge without following it.

Bring your attention, loosely, to the fact that your body is not engaging. This may show up as heaviness, numbness, blankness, tension, or absence. You do not need to locate it precisely. You do not need to stay with it continuously. You are simply acknowledging that something in you is not available.

If thoughts arise that try to explain the Freeze, such as "I should understand this," "This is unhealthy," or "I need to move through this," notice how your body responds to those thoughts. Often, the body tightens further in response to explanation. Let that tightening be part of what you notice.

You may quietly name, once or not at all: *This is a no*. There is no need to ask what the no is for.

Stay for as long as feels tolerable. If irritation, boredom, or restlessness arises, that does not mean the practice is failing. These are often the sensations that accompany refusal when productivity and meaning-making are suspended.

When you choose to end the practice, do so without a sense of completion. You are not closing the no. You are simply shifting your attention elsewhere.

Reflective Questions

As with all the reflective questions in this workbook, you may respond to any one question, more than one, or none at all. If your body says none at all, *no*, accept it. You can always come back another time.

- What was it like to stay with the "no" without moving toward explanation?
- What pressures arose to make the refusal meaningful or productive?
- How did your body respond to the idea of not resolving the Freeze?
- What does it mean for you to let a refusal remain incomplete?

Lived Experience: Salma

Salma has been exchanging messages with a family member about attending an upcoming event. The messages are polite but insistent. Each time she reads them, her stomach tightens and her chest feels heavy. She has not replied for two days. On the third day, she notices a familiar internal pressure: *I need to respond.* Rather than react to that pressure, she decides to sit with it instead.

She sits on her bed, phone face down beside her. Her body feels slow, almost stuck. Her shoulders slope forward. There is no clear emotion, just a dense sense of not wanting to engage. Several thoughts arise about being rude, irresponsible, ungrateful. Each time, her body seems to sink further into itself.

Instead of composing a response, Salma stays where she is. She does not rehearse what she might say later. She does not reassure herself that she will respond eventually. She simply lets the *no* be present. After some time, her body shifts slightly, but the no does not disappear. When she eventually stands up, the message is still unanswered. Nothing has been resolved. But Salma notices that she has not forced herself into a reply that would have cost her more than she could afford.

The refusal remains intact.

Summary

Freeze, as it is held in this chapter, is not absence, failure, or collapse. It is a bodily response that emerges when engagement itself becomes unsafe, costly, or extractive. Rather than understanding stillness, silence, numbness, or withdrawal as deficits to be corrected, Freeze: Refusal to Engage names these states as *precise forms of protest*, shaped by histories of punishment, erasure, surveillance, and constraint.

Freeze is not what happens when someone lacks strength, clarity, or resilience. It is what happens when the conditions required for participation are not present. For many marginalized bodies, speaking, explaining, or staying visible has repeatedly carried risk. Over time, the body learns where it cannot go and withdraws, not because it is powerless but because it refuses to continue offering itself to environments that do not hold safety or care.

In this frame, Freeze is not a step on the way to something else. It is not a stage to pass through or a problem to overcome. It is a complete response, grounded in discernment. The body does not disengage because it is weak; it disengages because engagement would come at too great a cost.

The work within this chapter is an orientation to the conditions that allow this work to be approached with integrity. Permission, pacing, and structural safety are central. Freeze cannot be explored ethically in spaces where silence is treated as disengagement, or where participants are expected to explain what their bodies are protecting. The invitation here is not toward activation or recovery. It is toward recognition, to let Freeze exist without pressure to make it productive, meaningful, or coherent.

Through the practices in this chapter, the invitation is to stay near the body without asking it to open, soften, or return to participation. Anchoring becomes a way of leaning on something steady while refusal remains. Reflection is framed not as self-analysis, but as witnessing the body's limits. Withholding engagement is approached as conscious non-participation. Staying with the no allows refusal to remain intact, without translating it into justification or repair.

Across the lived-experience vignettes, protest does not take the form of confrontation or assertion. It appears quietly; in silence after a meeting, in a message left unanswered, in the decision not to explain oneself again. Nothing is resolved. The environment does not change. What endures is an inner alignment: the body did not abandon itself in order to comply.

Freeze, in this chapter, is held with care and precision. It is not an obstacle to power or presence. It is a form of protection that emerges when survival, dignity, and limits must take precedence over participation. The work here is not to move past Freeze. It is to create conditions where Freeze does not have to work so hard to keep the self-intact and where its refusal can be met with recognition rather than demand.

How does "*Freeze*" make itself known in order to protect your body and keep your self-intact? Draw or write your reflections in this space...

Chapter 7

Coming Into My Power

Refusal to Be Erased

The previous chapter centered Freeze: Refusal To Engage as a complete and ethical form of protest. Freeze was not framed as something to overcome, soften, or move through. It was held as a bodily response shaped by material risk, survival, and the refusal to continue participating in conditions that demand erasure.

This chapter does not replace that understanding.

Coming Into My Power—Refusal To Be Erased is not what comes after Freeze. It is not a resolution, a recovery, or a return to capacity. Many bodies move between Freeze and thaw repeatedly. Some remain in Freeze for long periods. Some never leave it in the ways that are legible or rewarded. Nothing in this chapter suggests that Freeze must give way to something else. Instead, this chapter attends to moments when the body, under specific conditions, does not disappear.

Coming Into My Power—Refusal To Be Erased names those moments when a body stays present with itself, even while risk, constraint, or surveillance remains. It may show up as speaking, but it may also show up as staying, breathing, making eye contact, setting a boundary internally, or holding one's ground without display. What distinguishes this form of protest is not visibility, volume, or impact. It is the body's decision, however partial or temporary, not to vanish.

Erasure is not only about being silenced by others. It is also about the slow, cumulative pressure to shrink, comply, or disconnect from oneself in order to survive. Erasure happens when bodies learn that their anger is dangerous, their needs are excessive, their presence is conditional, or their truth must be softened to be tolerated.

For marginalized bodies, erasure is often enforced relationally. It happens in families, workplaces, institutions, classrooms, clinics, and communities. It is maintained through shame, politeness, urgency, and the demand to be "reasonable." Over time, these demands are taken into the body. They become habits of self-monitoring, self-doubt, and self-erasure.

Refusal To Be Erased does not undo these forces. It does not eliminate risk. What it does is interrupt the internal collapse that erasure relies on.

Refusal is often quiet. It may not be seen or rewarded. It may be followed by fear, grief, or exhaustion. It may last only a few seconds. But in those moments, the body remains in relationship with itself rather than abandoning itself to meet external demands.

DOI: 10.4324/9781003672203-10

Refusal To Be Erased is not resistance in the sense of confronting power or calling out injustice. That kind of resistance is not always possible or safe. Refusal To Be Erased is protest at the level of presence. It is the body saying: *I am still here*, even when disappearance would be easier, safer, or expected.

This presence does not require coherence or confidence. It does not require certainty or clarity. It may coexist with fear, trembling, anger, or doubt. What matters is not how well it is expressed, but that the body does not abandon itself in order to survive the moment.

In the earlier work on liberation, the body moved toward expansion and aliveness. In Freeze, the body withdrew to protect itself. Here, the body does something more ambiguous. It stays, but carefully. It remains, but selectively. It does not perform resilience or empowerment. It practices self-compassion as refusal.

In this chapter, self-compassion is not framed as soothing oneself or feeling better. It is framed as the refusal to internalize the logics of erasure. These logics tell marginalized bodies that suffering is personal, that harm is deserved, or that endurance is the price of belonging.

Self-compassion interrupts those logics by allowing the body to recognize its own suffering without turning against itself. It allows the body to see constraint without collapsing into shame. It makes room for anger, grief, and longing without demanding resolution. In this sense, self-compassion is not soft. It is protective. It allows the body to stay present without reproducing the violence it has already endured.

Coming Into My Power—Refusal To Be Erased is sustained not by confidence, but by care.

Conditions That Support Coming Into My Power—Refusal To Be Erased

Coming Into My Power does not arise through effort or intention alone. It emerges under particular conditions, and those conditions are often fragile, temporary, and unevenly available. Unlike liberation, which can sometimes be pursued deliberately, and unlike Freeze, which often arrives without choice, Coming Into My Power depends on whether the body senses that remaining present will not immediately result in harm.

Here, power does not mean confidence, control, or visibility. It refers to the body's capacity to remain in relationship with itself without collapsing into erasure. This capacity cannot be demanded, trained, or expected. It cannot be prescribed as a goal. The conditions that support it are not motivational. They are relational and structural.

One of the most important conditions is selectivity. Bodies that have survived erasure learn carefully where and with whom coming into power is possible. This does not happen everywhere at once. It may occur with one person and not another, in one setting and not another, around one topic and not another. This selectivity is not inconsistency. It is discernment shaped by lived experience.

Another condition is containment without pressure. Coming into my power is more likely when the body is not being asked to be coherent, articulate, or generous. When there is no expectation to explain oneself, justify one's reactions, or soften one's truth, the body may remain present for longer. Power collapses when presence is made useful to others.

Time also matters. Coming Into My Power often happens slowly, or in brief flashes. It may look like staying with a sensation for a few seconds longer than usual or not immediately overriding an inner response. It may look like delaying a reply, remaining in a room without speaking, or allowing an emotion to exist without correction. These are not small acts. They are measured responses to environments that have historically required disappearance.

Relational safety, when it exists, supports this work, but safety here does not mean comfort. It means predictability, consent, and the absence of punishment for being oneself. Even then, Coming Into My Power may still feel risky. The body may remain vigilant. Care does not remove fear. It allows fear to coexist with presence.

It is also important to name that Coming Into My Power is not always visible. It may not be recognized by others. It may not lead to change in the environment. Sometimes, it is known only to the body itself. This does not make it less real. For many marginalized bodies, the most significant refusals of erasure are the ones that remain unseen, because being witnessed has often carried risk.

Finally, Coming Into My Power is supported by self-compassion that does not rush repair. This includes allowing oneself to feel conflicted about staying present, to grieve what cannot be said, or to acknowledge the cost of remaining visible. Self-compassion here does not push toward empowerment or closure. It allows the body to stay in relationship with itself, even when the world remains unchanged.

Before moving into the practices in this chapter, you may want to pause and ask yourself quietly: *Where, if anywhere, does my body already refuse to disappear?*

The answer may be subtle.
It may not arrive in words.
It may arrive as a sensation, a limit, or a quiet steadiness.
That is enough.

Where, if anywhere, does my body already refuse to disappear?

Practice Invitation 1: Staying With Myself in the Moment of Contact

This practice is offered for moments when the body does not withdraw completely; yet, at the same time, does not feel free to expand. It attends to the subtle space where presence is possible without performance. In the context of Coming Into My Power—Refusal To Be Erased, power is not expressed through action or speech. It is expressed through staying in contact with oneself when erasure would be easier or expected.

Contact here does not mean connection with others. It refers to the body maintaining a thread of relationship with itself while being in proximity to a person, situation, or demand. This may happen in conversation, during conflict, while being watched, or when a response is anticipated. The practice does not ask you to speak, decide, or clarify. It asks only that you notice what it is like to remain internally present without disappearing.

Before beginning, choose a recent moment when you were in contact with someone or something and noticed the familiar pull to shrink, smooth over, or disconnect from yourself. This does not need to be a dramatic interaction. Ordinary moments often carry the clearest signals. If bringing the moment to mind feels too activating, you may choose a neutral or imagined situation instead.

Name the situation: ____

As you recall this moment, allow your body to orient in whatever way feels most supportive. You might be sitting, standing, or lying down. There is no instruction to relax or ground. Let your body be as it is.

Notice first whether there is a sense of contact anywhere. This might feel like a steady pressure, a line of sensation, a place of warmth, or even a sense of holding on. It might also feel faint or intermittent. You are not trying to strengthen it. You are simply noticing whether it exists.

As you stay with this contact, you may become aware of impulses to leave yourself. These might include urges to appease, to explain, to dissociate slightly, to agree too quickly, or to move on internally. Rather than following or resisting these impulses, notice what it is like to stay with yourself for just one or two breaths longer than usual. This staying does not require clarity. You do not need to know what you want or what you will do next. The practice is complete if, for even a brief moment, you remain present with your own sensations while the pull toward erasure is active.

If fear, tension, or shakiness arises, that does not mean the practice is failing. These sensations often accompany moments of power when power is understood as *not disappearing*. You are welcome to end the practice at any time, especially if remaining present begins to feel unsafe.

When you are ready to finish, allow your attention to shift gently back to your surroundings. There is no need to close the practice with meaning or insight. Staying with yourself, even briefly, is enough.

Take a moment to note down your experience of this practice...

Reflective Questions

As a way of deepening this practice, we invite you to respond to one or more of the following questions. Remember, choosing not to do this step of the practice is also welcome—the invitation will remain here if, and when, you feel ready to return.

- What helped you stay in contact with yourself, even briefly?
- What impulses toward erasure did you notice?
- How did your body respond to staying present without knowing what to do next?
- In what ways did this moment feel different from both freezing and expanding?

Lived Experience: Riya

Riya is in a conversation with a colleague who is questioning a decision Riya made earlier in the week. The tone is polite but pointed. As the colleague speaks, Riya notices a familiar sensation in her body, a slight hollowing in her chest, a sense of pulling inward. She recognizes this as the beginning of her usual response: agreeing quickly, minimizing her own reasoning, and moving the conversation along.

As the colleague pauses, waiting for a response, Riya feels the pressure to smooth things over. Instead of answering immediately, she notices her feet on the ground. The sensation is faint, but present. Her breath feels shallow. There is tension in her jaw. She does not yet know what she wants to say. She does not feel confident. She feels exposed.

For a few seconds, Riya stays with the sensation of her feet, with the tightness in her jaw, with the awareness that she is still here. The colleague is watching her. The silence stretches slightly. Eventually, Riya does speak, but the content of what she says is less important than what happened before. In that brief pause, she did not leave herself. She did not disappear in order to keep the interaction comfortable.

Later, when she thinks back on the moment, Riya does not feel triumphant. She feels tired. But she also notices that she remembers the conversation clearly. She did not lose time. She did not go blank. Something in her remained intact.

That, for her, is what coming into power looked like that day.

Practice Invitation 2: Allowing the Boundary to Exist Without Enforcing It

This practice attends to moments when a boundary is present in the body, even if it is not spoken, enacted, or defended. In the context of Coming Into My Power, power does not always appear as setting limits or asserting needs outwardly. For many marginalized bodies, enforcing a boundary can invite retaliation, withdrawal of care, or increased scrutiny. In such moments, the body may choose to hold a boundary internally.

Allowing the boundary to exist without enforcing it is not resignation. It is a way of staying aligned with oneself when external enforcement would come at too great a cost.

This practice supports the body in recognizing its own limits without requiring them to become action.

Before beginning, choose a recent situation where you sensed a boundary internally but did not express it. This might have been a moment when you wanted to say no, slow something down, ask for space, or stop a conversation, but did not. The focus here is not on what you should have done differently. It is on what your body already knew.

Name the situation: ____

As you bring this moment to mind, notice what happens in your body. You might feel a tightening, a pulling back, a heaviness, or a quiet firmness. You may also notice uncertainty or ambivalence. Let these sensations be present without labeling them as right or wrong.

Instead of asking how to communicate the boundary, see if you can stay with the fact that the boundary exists. You might quietly acknowledge, *something in me has a limit here*. There is no need to define the limit clearly. Many boundaries are felt before they can be named.

As you remain with this sensing, notice any internal pressure to justify the boundary, soften it, or make it reasonable. You may also notice fear about what would happen if the boundary were known. These responses are not obstacles to the practice. They are part of the context in which the boundary formed. Allow the boundary to remain unexpressed for the duration of the practice. This is not avoidance. It is a recognition that internal alignment matters, even when external alignment is not possible. Staying with the boundary, rather than overriding it, is itself a form of refusal to be erased.

When you are ready to end the practice, let your attention return to your surroundings. There is nothing to decide or resolve. The boundary does not need to be acted on for it to be real.

Reflection Prompts

(You may respond to any one question, more than one, or none at all.)

- Where did you sense the boundary in your body, if at all?
- What pressures arose to explain, soften, or override it?
- How did it feel to let the boundary exist without acting on it?
- In what ways might this internal boundary be an expression of power rather than passivity?

____

____

____

____

____

____

> **Lived Experience: Devika**
>
> Devika is visiting extended family for a holiday. During a conversation after dinner, a relative makes a comment about her life choices, framed as concern. The tone is familiar. Devika feels a tightening in her stomach and a heaviness settle across her chest. She knows this moment. It is the point where she usually explains herself, offers context, or jokes to ease the tension.
>
> As the comment lands, Devika notices a clear internal response: *I don't want to go into this*. The boundary is immediate and bodily. Her shoulders draw in slightly. Her breath becomes shallow. She does not say anything right away. She nods once, non-committal. The conversation moves on. On the outside, it may look like she has let the comment pass. Inside, something different is happening. She is aware of the boundary and chooses not to abandon it by arguing herself into justification.
>
> Later that evening, as she sits alone in her room, Devika returns to the moment. She notices that while she did not speak up, she also did not collapse into self-doubt in the way she often does. The boundary had remained intact, even without enforcement.
>
> Nothing about the family dynamic has changed. The comment still stings. But Devika recognizes that she did not erase herself to keep the peace. For her, that quiet internal alignment is what coming into power looks like in that context.

Practice Invitation 3: Staying With Discomfort Without Self-Betrayal

This practice supports moments when discomfort arises and the familiar response is to turn against oneself in order to make the situation easier, smoother, or more acceptable to others. In the context of Coming Into My Power, power is not the absence of discomfort. It is the capacity to stay with discomfort without converting it into self-blame, self-doubt, or self-erasure.

For many marginalized bodies, discomfort has been repeatedly reframed as personal inadequacy. Anger becomes "too much," sadness becomes "unprofessional," hesitation becomes "lack of confidence." Over time, the body learns to manage discomfort by questioning itself rather than the conditions that produce the discomfort. This practice interrupts that reflex.

Before beginning, choose a moment when discomfort was present and you noticed an impulse to judge yourself for it. This might include feeling upset in a meeting, feeling tense in a conversation, or feeling overwhelmed by an expectation. You do not need to choose a moment of crisis. Subtle discomfort is often enough.

Name the situation: ____

As you bring this moment to mind, notice how discomfort shows up in your body. You may feel heat, tightness, restlessness, heaviness, or agitation. You may also feel emotionally flat. Let whatever is present be present, without naming it as a problem.

Next, notice whether any self-directed judgments arise alongside the discomfort. These may sound like "I'm overreacting," "I should handle this better," or "This shouldn't bother me." Rather than trying to counter these thoughts, notice how your body responds when they appear. Often, the discomfort intensifies when self-betrayal begins.

If it feels possible, see what it is like to let the discomfort exist without adding interpretation. This does not mean liking it or understanding it. It means not immediately using it as evidence against yourself. You might quietly acknowledge, *something in me is uncomfortable, and that does not mean I am wrong*. You do not need to repeat this or convince yourself. One recognition is enough.

Stay with this experience for as long as feels tolerable. If the discomfort shifts, intensifies, or fades, allow that to happen without commentary. If staying becomes too much, you are welcome to end the practice at any time. Ending early is a form of care, not avoidance.

When you are ready to close, return your attention to your surroundings. The discomfort does not need to resolve for the practice to be complete.

Reflection Prompts

(*You may respond to any one question, more than one, or none at all.*)

- What forms of discomfort felt most familiar in this practice?
- What self-directed judgments tended to arise alongside the discomfort?
- How did your body respond when you did not immediately side with those judgments?
- In what way might staying with discomfort, without self-betrayal, be an expression of power?

____
____
____
____
____
____

Lived Experience: Karthik

Karthik is part of a planning meeting at work. As timelines are discussed, he feels a growing tension in his chest. The deadlines feel unrealistic, but no one else is naming it. As the conversation continues, a familiar thought appears: *Everyone else seems fine. Why am I struggling with this?* He notices the tension increase as that thought settles in. His shoulders tighten. His breathing becomes shallow. In the past, this is where he would disengage internally, telling himself to push through and stop making a big deal out of things.

This time, Karthik stays with the sensation instead. He does not speak. He does not interrupt the meeting. But he notices the discomfort without turning it into evidence of personal inadequacy. The tension remains, but it no longer feels fused with shame.

After the meeting ends, Karthik feels tired. The discomfort has not disappeared. But later, as he reflects on the moment, he realizes that he did not abandon himself to maintain the appearance of ease. He did not convince himself that the pressure was imaginary. The meeting has not changed. The deadlines remain. What has shifted is his relationship to his own discomfort. It now feels like information rather than accusation.

For him, that shift is part of coming into power.

Practice Invitation 4: Letting Presence Be Enough

This practice attends to moments when the body remains present without taking action, setting boundaries, or making meaning. In Coming Into My Power, presence itself is not a step toward something else. It is not preparation for expression, change, or repair. It is a refusal to disappear when disappearance has been the safer or more familiar option.

For many marginalized bodies, presence has often been conditional. One can remain present only if one is agreeable, useful, coherent, or easy to be with. Over time, the body learns to withdraw presence as a way of staying safe. This practice invites a different possibility: remaining present without offering explanation, reassurance, or performance.

Before beginning, choose a recent moment where you stayed physically present in a situation but felt yourself slipping away internally. This might have happened during a conversation, a meeting, a family interaction, or a public space where you felt watched. The practice is not about changing what you did in that moment. It is about noticing what it is like to let presence exist on its own terms.

Name the situation: ____

As you bring the moment to mind, notice whether your body feels here or distant. Presence may feel thin, tentative, or intermittent. You may sense it as a quiet steadiness, a subtle alertness, or simply the absence of complete withdrawal. You are not trying to deepen or stabilize this presence. You are acknowledging that it exists at all.

As you stay with this sensing, notice any pressure to *do something* with your presence. This might include urges to speak, to justify yourself, to appear calm, or to demonstrate engagement. Rather than following or resisting these urges, notice how your body responds to the idea that presence does not need to be productive.

If fear, self-consciousness, or fatigue arises, allow it to be there. Presence in these moments is not comfortable. It often carries cost. This practice does not remove that cost. It simply names presence as sufficient, even when it feels exposed or incomplete.

You may stay with this for a few moments, or longer if it feels supportive. When you are ready to end, allow your attention to return to your surroundings. There is no closure required. Presence does not need to lead anywhere to matter.

Reflection Prompts

(*You may respond to any one question, more than one, or none at all.*)

- How did presence show up in your body during this practice, if at all?
- What pressures arose to make your presence useful, visible, or reassuring?
- What was it like to let presence exist without action or explanation?
- In what ways might presence itself function as a refusal of erasure?

____
____
____
____
____
____
____
____
____
____
____
____
____
____
____

Lived Experience: Priya

Priya is sitting in a classroom during a discussion that brushes close to her own lived experience, though no one names it directly. The conversation moves on without pause. She feels a familiar pull to disappear, to become smaller, to let the moment pass without registering inside her.

Instead, Priya notices that she remains seated, her back against the chair, her feet on the floor. Her body feels alert, slightly tense. She does not raise her hand. She does not interrupt. She also does not drift away. There is a moment when she wonders if she should be doing more, saying more. The thought passes. What remains is the sensation of being here, even as the discussion continues around her.

Later, when the class ends, Priya feels drained. The experience was not affirming. Nothing in the room changed. But she notices that she remembers the discussion clearly. She did not lose herself in the way she sometimes does.

For Priya, coming into power that day did not mean speaking up or being recognized. It meant staying present without erasing herself in order to get through the moment.

Summary

Coming Into My Power, as it has been held in this chapter, is not a destination. It is not a stable state, a new identity, or an achievement that can be claimed and kept. It appears in moments, often briefly, often quietly, and often at cost. It may not be visible to others. It may not change the conditions that made erasure likely in the first place.

What it does is interrupt disappearance.

Across the practices in this chapter, power has been approached as the body's capacity to remain in relationship with itself under pressure. This has included staying present without clarity, allowing boundaries to exist without enforcement, holding discomfort without self-betrayal, and letting presence be enough without turning it into action or explanation. None of these require confidence. None of them guarantees safety. All of them are shaped by context.

This understanding of power resists the idea that marginalized bodies must always move outward, speak louder, or become more visible in order to be whole. It also resists the idea that power only counts when it produces change that others can see. For many bodies, the most meaningful refusals of erasure are internal, relational, and known only to the self.

Coming Into My Power does not replace Freeze. It does not undo it. Many bodies move back and forth between Refusal to Engage and Refusal to be Erased, depending on the conditions of the moment. Sometimes, Freeze remains the most protective response. Sometimes, presence becomes possible. Neither is more evolved than the other.

What matters is not which response appears, but whether the body is met with recognition rather than demand.

As you close this chapter, you are not asked to carry these practices forward or to apply them consistently. You are invited only to notice where, if anywhere, your body already refuses to disappear, even briefly. That noticing, in itself, is part of the work.

Power, in this frame, is not something you take.
It is something you allow to exist, without erasing yourself to earn it.

How do you witness "*Coming Into My Power*" revealing itself in your body? Draw or write your reflections in this space…

Part IV

Body as a Site of Resistance

What comes to mind when you read the phrase "*Body as a Site of Resistance*"? Draw or write your reflections in this space...

DOI: 10.4324/9781003672203-11

In this workbook, resistance is not treated as a single thing or a moral stance. It is approached as a layered bodily process that becomes visible when awareness, movement, or change meets protection. Resistance is what happens when the body senses that something needs to shift and, at the same time, feels invested in keeping things the same.

Chapters 8 and 9 use the term resistance primarily to describe how bodies shaped by systemic privilege respond when dominant arrangements are unsettled. Systemic privilege does not mean an easy life, moral failure, or freedom from harm. It refers to forms of structural insulation—conditions in which certain bodies are more likely to be protected from the consequences of injustice, believed when they speak, allowed distance from harm, or granted the option to disengage. Privilege is always relative, contextual, and uneven, and many people live at mixed locations; for example, someone may be upper-caste and economically secure while living with neurodivergence, transness, disability, or chronic illness. These mixed locations matter. They shape how much a body must endure, how much it can adapt, and how much it is allowed not to notice.

Because privilege is relational, resistance does not look the same across bodies. For marginalized bodies living under precarity, what this workbook names as protest emerges as the body's response to harm—through freeze, refusal, silence, withdrawal, or survival strategies that protect dignity in unsafe conditions. For bodies positioned closer to systemic power, resistance often appears differently. It shows up when awareness of inequality begins to form and the body responds by defending comfort, innocence, normalcy, or familiarity.

In the language of physics, resistance describes what happens when energy meets impedance—when movement generates friction, heat, or slowing. Applied to the body, resistance appears as tension, defensiveness, urgency, fatigue, explanation, withdrawal, or intellectualization. These are not personal failures. They are signals of where the body is working to protect an existing arrangement that has offered some safety, status, or distance from harm. That protection is not neutral. What is preserved here is often sustained through the unequal distribution of risk, labor, or silence elsewhere, and the body is meeting that friction of safety and the inequity of it.

Psychoanalytic traditions name resistance as the body's defense against destabilizing awareness. When long-held assumptions about neutrality, merit, or exemption are challenged, the body may delay, rationalize, deflect, or look away because something familiar is being threatened. The body is negotiating the loss of certainty before it may move toward accountability, and sometimes in order to avoid that movement altogether.

Social justice traditions have used the word resistance to name the active opposition of marginalized communities against oppressive systems. In this workbook, that meaning is not discarded. Instead, it is approached as something that privileged bodies must grow into. Collective resistance does not emerge simply from knowing, feeling discomfort, or holding good intentions. It emerges when bodily impulses—defense, hesitation, explanation, collapse—are met with curiosity, responsibility, and relationship, and are gradually reoriented toward shared accountability and action, including the redistribution of comfort, attention, and cost.

Seen this way, resistance is not an endpoint. It is a threshold. Thresholds ask something of the body. They are places where staying begins to reorganize responsibility, not just awareness. When the body's friction is stayed with rather than bypassed, it can become the ground from which ethical, collective resistance takes shape—not as reaction or self-blame, but as commitment to liberation beyond the self. When the body recognizes how it has been positioned, what it has been shielded from, and what it has absorbed without question, resistance can shift from protecting comfort to joining hands in solidarity.

A Note About Practices in This Section

The practices in the next two chapters build on the somatic language, pacing, and ethical orientation developed across the earlier sections of this workbook. By the time you arrive here, it is assumed that you will have some familiarity with noticing bodily responses, staying with sensation, and relating personal experience to structural conditions of caste, race, class, gender, disability, queerness, and other axes of power. If you are coming to Chapters 8 and 9 first, and you find that the invitations here feel more demanding of your body or less clearly scaffolded, you are welcome to linger, move slowly, or dip back into earlier chapters whenever your body signals the need for more grounding or context.

Body as a Site of Resistance asks something specific of the reader: to notice how the body is also shaped by protection, insulation, and exemption. This can be unsettling work. It often brings people into contact with friction, defensiveness, grief, shame, confusion, or fatigue. These responses are not signs of failure or lack of commitment. They are signs that the body is encountering the limits of familiar ways of seeing oneself and one's role in systems of power.

Given the nature of this work, the practices in the following two chapters are designed to be approached slowly, with choice and with attention to capacity. They are not meant to be completed in one sitting, nor are they meant to be performed at moments of acute overwhelm or burnout. Resistance work that bypasses the body's limits often reproduces the very logics of extraction and endurance that justice movements are trying to undo. You are encouraged to stop, adapt, or return to earlier practices whenever fatigue, shutdown, or overwhelm signals that your capacity has been reached.

Working with privilege, complicity, and resistance can be emotionally and somatically demanding, particularly for people who already live at mixed or precarious locations within systems of power. These practices are, therefore, offered as supports for sustainability, not as tests of moral readiness or political correctness. They are not intended to replace activism, organizing, or material redistribution. Rather, they support the kinds of bodily awareness that make long-term engagement possible without collapse, righteousness, or withdrawal. When practiced with care, they can help people notice when their activism is being driven by urgency, guilt, or a need to remain innocent, and when it is being shaped by accountability, relationship, and shared responsibility.

Somatic work here is not an alternative to action. It is a way of staying with action over time.

These practices are offered for individual reflection and can also be taken up in collective spaces such as therapy groups, supervision settings, peer circles, classrooms, or community gatherings. Practicing together can deepen learning when the space is intentionally shaped to support slowness, consent, confidentiality, and the right to pause, step back, or opt out without explanation. Because the next two chapters work directly with friction, privilege, and resistance, collective practice is often most generative when participants share some proximity of privilege in the domain being explored, whether that is caste, race, class, professional authority, citizenship, or ability, so that accountability does not fall on those already carrying greater risk or exposure. When groups are mixed, facilitators carry an ethical responsibility to actively attend to power, to prevent marginalized participants from being positioned as educators or sites of extraction, and to interrupt patterns of justification, confession, or emotional offloading that recenter dominant comfort.

These practices are not designed for public processing, moral display, or resolution in a single sitting. They work best in spaces where discomfort is met with curiosity rather than urgency; where silence is allowed; and where responsibility is understood as relational, ongoing, and shaped over time. Attended to in this way, collective practice supports sustainable engagement rather than burnout, and deepens social justice activism rather than replacing it. Resistance here becomes a shared capacity to stay present, responsive, and accountable as dominant arrangements are unsettled, in service of widening the possibilities for protest, liberation, and collective change.

When Pacing Becomes Protection

Choice and pacing are essential to this work. They are also not neutral. For bodies that have been structurally protected from consequence, moving slowly can sometimes function as a way of holding onto comfort rather than building sustainability. We invite you to notice when pacing supports your capacity to stay, and when it quietly postpones responsibility.

Further, these practices invite you to move slowly, with care and choice, because the work of resistance requires bodies that can stay present without collapse or hardening. At the same time, slowness and self-tending are not neutral. For bodies shaped by relative safety, credibility, or protection, care can support accountability, and it can also quietly restore comfort without changing what is held in place. As you engage these practices, you are invited to notice not only what helps you stay, but what your pacing makes possible, what it postpones, and what responsibility remains waiting. The intention here is not to rush the body or override consent, but to situate care within power, so that awareness does not become a substitute for change.

Chapter 8

Friction with Privilege

As awareness of systemic privilege begins to form, the body often responds before the mind knows what to do. This response is rarely calm or clear. It may appear as restlessness, nausea, heaviness, agitation, lethargy, shame, confusion, or a sense of being stuck. In this workbook, this phase is named Friction with Privilege.

Friction with Privilege describes what happens when the body senses the contradictions of advantage. It is the strain of recognizing that access, safety, credibility, or choice have been unevenly distributed, and that one's own body has been shaped by this unevenness. This recognition does not arrive as clarity or resolve. It arrives as bodily tension.

For many people, this friction emerges through relative privilege. A person may experience caste, race, or class advantage alongside gendered, religious, disability-based, or linguistic marginalization. Privilege is not an all-or-nothing position. It is layered, contextual, and relational. This is why friction often feels confusing. The body is holding more than one truth at once.

What truths are your body holding? Take a moment to name some of your experienced layers that shape your *"Body as a Site of Resistance"*...

DOI: 10.4324/9781003672203-12

Friction is not yet resistance. It is the moment where the body begins to register that something does not align but has not yet reorganized itself toward responsibility or action. At this stage, bodies often explain, delay, intellectualize, feel ashamed, or withdraw. These responses are not moral failures. They are protective patterns shaped by socialization.

The danger of Friction with Privilege is not discomfort itself, but avoidance. When bodily unease is bypassed or collapsed into guilt, the system remains untouched. When friction is stayed with, without centering shame or seeking relief, it becomes a threshold. It is here that the body begins to learn how to remain present in discomfort without reintegrating into dominance.

The practices in this chapter support you to stay with friction without rushing to resolve it. They do not ask you to fix yourself, justify your access, or perform allyship. Instead, they invite you to notice how privilege is lived in the body, how it is defended, and how it can be reoriented toward ethical responsibility.

This is not yet collective resistance.

It is the necessary ground from which resistance can grow.

Practice Invitation 1: Somatic Inquiry into Friction with Privilege

This practice supports noticing how privilege is registered in the body before it becomes thought, action, or explanation. Friction often appears as bodily discomfort when privilege becomes visible in relational, institutional, or everyday contexts. Rather than moving away from this discomfort, the practice invites you to stay close to it.

The intention is not to absolve, justify, or correct. It is to listen. Friction is treated as information about where the body is protecting familiarity, belonging, or innocence, even as it senses misalignment.

You may take 15–20 minutes for this practice. Choose a space where you can sit without interruption. Keep water nearby. If strong emotions arise, orient to your surroundings, name objects in the room, or pause. **You are allowed to stop at any point**. You may also notice what becomes easier when you stop, and what responsibility remains waiting.

Before beginning, remind yourself: *Discomfort is information. I do not need to resolve it.*

Take a few breaths if that is possible. Notice contact with the ground or the surface supporting you.

Let your body arrive as it is, without trying to calm it.

The Practice

Bring to mind a recent moment where you noticed privilege operating in your life. This could be an instance of access, ease, deference, protection, or being believed, especially in contrast to someone else.

Name the situation: ____

As you recall the moment, notice what happens in your body. Do not analyze yet.

Choose one sensation that feels most present. It may be tightness, heat, restlessness, heaviness, numbness, or something harder to name. Stay with this sensation for a few breaths. You might quietly name it.

Name the sensation: ____

Then gently ask the sensation:

- *What are you trying to protect right now?*
- *What feels at risk if I stay with this awareness?*

Notice what arises. You do not need a clear answer.

____
____
____
____
____
____

After a few moments, ask:

- *What value or truth is beginning to press for attention here?*

____
____
____
____
____
____

Let the practice end when your body signals enough.

Reflection Prompts

These prompts are designed to support your deepening into the practice. Remember, you are in control of how you move through this workbook, so you can choose one or more question or skip this section entirely. The choice is yours. Honor your body in this moment.

- What bodily sensations tend to signal friction for me?
- How do I usually respond to this discomfort?
- What becomes possible when I stay with it instead of resolving it?
- What might this friction be asking me to learn before I act?

Lived Experience: Anjali

Anjali joined a small peer circle that met monthly to practice somatic inquiry around power, identity, and accountability. The group was composed of other upper-caste professionals, all of whom had chosen to work specifically with caste and workplace privilege. The facilitator named the agreement clearly at the start: *this was a space not for confession or reassurance, but for noticing how the body responds when familiar arrangements are unsettled.*

During the session on Somatic Inquiry into Friction with Privilege, participants were invited to bring to mind a recent moment where something felt off but had gone unnamed. Anjali's memory surfaced quickly. A work meeting from earlier that week. A queer colleague had been interrupted multiple times while speaking. Anjali had noticed it in the moment. She had even felt a flicker of irritation. But she had stayed quiet, watching as her own suggestions were taken up without interruption.

As the group settled into silence, Anjali felt a familiar dull heaviness spread across her chest, accompanied by a sinking sensation in her stomach. The facilitator reminded everyone to stay with one sensation, without analysis, and to ask gently what it might be protecting. When Anjali posed the question inwardly, the response came almost immediately: "*If you speak, you will be seen as rude.*" Her body recognized this rule. It was old. Being accommodating, respectful, and "not difficult" had been praised throughout her childhood. Goodness, in her body, had learned to mean quiet endurance.

As the practice continued, the group was invited to notice if other layers emerged. Anjali felt the heaviness deepen; not intensify, but widen. What surfaced next surprised her. The sensation was not only about gendered expectations. It was about caste safety. She realized that her ability to remain silent without consequence was not accidental. Her body could afford moral ease because the harm was not directed at her. Caste had insulated her. Neutrality was available to her in ways it was not to her colleague.

When it came time to share, Anjali spoke briefly, naming only what felt steady. She did not explain or justify. She said, "*My body learned that silence keeps me good. Today I noticed that this goodness is protected by caste.*" No one rushed to respond. The facilitator simply thanked her for naming it.

Nothing resolved in that session. There was no collective affirmation, no plan of action, no pressure to promise change. But something shifted in how Anjali related to the sensation itself. In the weeks that followed, similar moments arose at work. The heaviness returned, but sooner. This time, Anjali did not mistake it for personal hesitation or politeness. She recognized it as friction with privilege. Her body signaling a familiar protection pattern.

The practice had not made her fearless. It had made her oriented.

Later, reflecting in her journal, Anjali wrote: "*I used to think discomfort meant I was doing something wrong. Now I see that it often means my body is protecting an arrangement that benefits me. Staying with that feeling helps me choose differently.*"

For Anjali, the group did not provide answers. It provided conditions. A place where bodily resistance could be noticed without collapse or performance. Where silence could be understood not as virtue, but as information. And where the work of resistance began not with certainty, but with staying present as moral innocence loosened its grip.

This naming did not resolve the friction. But it changed her relationship to it. The body was no longer just absorbing. It was beginning to notice.

Practice Invitation 2: Body Scan for Complicity and Discomfort

This practice begins by anchoring the body in a real moment where awareness of power, privilege, or inequality has already been stirred—even subtly. Before starting the body scan, bring to mind one situation from your recent life where something felt uneasy, charged, or slightly off, but perhaps not fully named.

This could be:

- a conversation where you noticed yourself explaining, minimizing, or staying silent
- a news story about caste, religion, disability, gender, labor, war, or state violence that you quickly scrolled past or felt overwhelmed by
- a policy update, social media post, or public debate that made you feel defensive, tired, numb, or irritated
- a workplace, family, or community moment where inequality was visible, but you felt unsure how to respond
- a moment where you benefited from ease, access, or protection while knowing others did not

You are not choosing a moment to analyze or judge.

You are simply choosing a moment where your body already registered something, even if your mind moved on.

Let the situation remain lightly in the background, like a distant image or atmosphere, rather than replaying it in detail. The practice is not about the event itself, but about how your body holds what it could not yet act on, name, or resolve.

Name the situation: ____

Once you have this reference, allow your attention to turn inward and begin the body scan.

This is a practice of staying present at the edge where awareness meets protection. Choose a quiet, supported space where you can sit or lie down comfortably for about 15–20 minutes. You may wish to keep a notebook nearby, though writing is optional.

Before beginning, identify a gentle anchor. This might be the contact of your feet with the floor, your back against the chair, or the rhythm of your breath.

Name the anchor: ____

Remind yourself that you are not here to judge your body, fix it, or extract insight quickly. For bodies shaped by relative protection, slowness can support accountability, and it can also restore comfort. This practice invites noticing which one is happening.

You might quietly say to yourself: *I am practicing awareness, not punishment.*

You are free to pause, open your eyes, shift position, or stop at any time.

The Practice

Begin a slow body scan, moving at your own pace. You might start at the head and move downward, or begin wherever your attention naturally goes.

As you scan, notice areas that feel tense, dull, heavy, guarded, or absent. When you encounter such a place, pause there. Rather than trying to relax it, stay with the sensation.

Gently ask, without demanding an answer: *What might this part of my body be holding in relation to power, advantage, or comfort?*

You might notice images, memories, roles, explanations, or nothing at all. All of this is welcome.

If it feels supportive, you can ask one more question: *What does this part of me believe it needs to protect or preserve?*

Let the sensation remain as it is. You are not trying to dissolve it.

Breathe into the space around it, as if making room for it to be felt.

As you continue the scan, also notice areas that feel grounded, open, or at ease.

Ask: *What conditions allow ease here? Who has access to this ease, and who might not?*

Toward the end of the scan, bring your attention to your whole body as a field. Notice how discomfort and ease coexist.

Allow the practice to close with one steady breath.

Post-Practice Reflection

After your practice you may choose to spend some time reflecting on one or more of the following questions:

- Where did I notice discomfort or resistance most clearly in my body?
- What did that sensation seem to be protecting or preserving?
- How do ease and discomfort coexist in my body, and how might that reflect my social positioning?
- What would it mean to stay with this sensation longer in real interactions, rather than explaining or escaping it?

Remember, do not rush this process, you can always come back and revisit these prompts at any time you feel resourced to do so.

Discomfort around privilege is not something to overcome quickly.

It is the place where responsibility begins to take shape.

When the body learns that it can remain present with tension, without collapsing into shame or hardening into defense, resistance becomes possible. Not resistance as denial, but resistance as staying, listening, and allowing awareness to change how power is held.

Lived Experience: Kishore

Kishore, a cis man from a dominant caste background, noticed that discussions about gender and caste justice often left him feeling inexplicably tight in the chest. He described himself as supportive of equality, yet something in his body reacted before he could think. During the Body Scan for Complicity and Discomfort, his attention kept returning to that tightness. Instead of pushing past it, he stayed. When he asked what it was protecting, a quiet recognition surfaced. The tension was guarding his sense of being "*one of the good ones*," someone who did not want his comfort questioned.

As he breathed with the sensation, he realized how quickly he moved to agreement in conversations, not as solidarity but as a way to avoid deeper discomfort. The tightness did not disappear. But it changed shape. It became a signal rather than an obstacle.

In later conversations, Kishore began to notice that same sensation arise just before he explained himself or spoke over others. Remembering the practice, he learned to pause instead. The body scan did not make him less uncomfortable. It helped him stay present long enough for accountability to become possible.

Practice Invitation 3: Attending to Everyday Friction

Friction with Privilege does not only appear in explicit conflict or confrontation. More often, it shows up quietly in everyday relational rhythms—who speaks first, who is expected to adjust, who is given time, who is interrupted, who explains, who is believed, who absorbs discomfort so that others remain at ease.

This practice invites you to notice how your body participates in these ordinary moments. Rather than analyzing behavior or judging intention, you attend to bodily responses as they arise in daily interactions. The body often senses imbalance, entitlement, avoidance, or over-responsibility before the mind names it. By staying with these sensations, you begin to recognize how privilege moves through habit, pace, tone, and expectation.

This is a practice of resistance because it interrupts automatic participation in relational patterns that maintain inequality. For bodies shaped by relative safety or authority, slowing down, stepping back, or choosing not to act are not neutral gestures. This practice invites noticing when ease, restraint, or invisibility are already supported by power. The aim is not to correct yourself in the moment, but to build bodily awareness of how power lives in the everyday—and how it might be met differently.

Choose a day when your interactions are relatively ordinary, especially moments that feel smooth, easy, or unremarkable—work, family, community, online spaces, public places. This practice unfolds in real time, but reflection happens later.

Remind yourself: *noticing is enough for this practice*. You are not required to intervene, explain, or repair immediately.

If at any point you feel overwhelmed, return to grounding. Perhaps feel your feet, name objects around you, or take a few steady breaths.

At the start of the day, hold this gentle orientation: *Today, I am noticing how my body responds in ordinary interactions.*

You do not need to remember this all day. Let it return whenever it can.

The Practice

As you move through the day, notice moments such as: speaking in a meeting, waiting or not waiting, being interrupted or interrupting, giving advice, receiving appreciation or criticism, choosing whether to engage or stay silent, moving through public spaces, reading or hearing news, participating in family or community routines or other ordinary relational moments that quietly position you closer to safety, authority, distance, or choice.

When one such moment catches your attention, pause internally and notice:

- What happens in my body right now? Tightening, ease, urgency, heaviness, relaxation, withdrawal, alertness?
- Does my body move toward comfort, explanation, control, avoidance, or speed?
- Is there an impulse to smooth things over, dominate, rescue, disengage, or justify?

You do not need to change anything. Simply register the bodily signal.

Later, perhaps at a time when you can pause and be with yourself, choose one moment to reflect on. Ask yourself:

- What was being asked of me in that moment—explicitly or implicitly?
- What did my body already know about fairness, imbalance, or responsibility?
- How might privilege have shaped my ease, speed, authority, or invisibility there?

Let the reflection remain unfinished. The practice is about learning the body's language, not arriving at conclusions.

Use this space to capture your practice as it unfolded in your day…

Reflection Prompts

To extend this practice, you may choose one of the following prompts to journal or skip this reflection entirely.

- In what everyday moments does my body signal ease, urgency, or entitlement?
- What relational patterns feel "normal" to me, and who might they advantage or burden?
- How does my body respond when I slow down or step back, even slightly?
- How is my body learning resistance as a practice of responsibility, rather than opposition?

Remember, resistance, in this chapter, is not dramatic refusal. It is the capacity to notice how privilege reproduces itself through ordinary rhythms, and to stay present long enough for awareness to form. When the body learns to sense these patterns without collapsing into shame or denial, it becomes capable of more ethical movement later. This practice builds the somatic ground from which accountability, repair, and solidarity can emerge.

Lived Experience: Leela

Leela works in a nonprofit team that values openness. During weekly check-ins, she often speaks early and at length, offering reflections and suggestions. She considers herself thoughtful and engaged. One afternoon, during a routine meeting, she noticed a slight tightness in her jaw as she began speaking, a familiar sensation she usually ignored. Remembering the practice, she stayed with it silently. She realized her body was bracing, as if to secure her place before someone else did.

Later that evening, she reflected on the moment. She recognized how her caste and educational privilege had shaped a sense of entitlement to airtime, even in spaces committed to equality. The tightness wasn't guilt; it was awareness arriving before habit shifted.

The next meeting, Leela didn't force herself to be silent. Instead, she waited for her body to settle before speaking. She noticed others entering the conversation differently. Nothing dramatic changed, but something important loosened. Her body had begun teaching her how privilege lives in rhythm, not just belief.

Practice Invitation 4: The Pause That Disrupts Power

This practice explores how urgency, speed, and continuity are often shaped into privilege bodies, even when our intentions are ethical. Many systems of caste, race, class, gender, ability, and productivity rely on certain bodies continuing without pause, while others absorb the cost.

Friction with Privilege often becomes visible not in what we say, but in how quickly we move, how little we stop, and whose exhaustion we fail to notice. This practice invites you to meet the moment when the body wants to rush, override, explain, or push through and pause there.

The pause here is not a technique for calm.
It is a way of interrupting inherited momentum.

By staying with the bodily discomfort that arises when we slow down, this practice helps reveal how power travels through time, pace, and expectation and how resistance begins when that flow is gently disrupted.

You may take 5–10 minutes, once or multiple times in a day.

Choose an ordinary moment, not a crisis. This practice works best inside daily rhythms—work, caregiving, conversations, planning, scrolling, responding.

Before beginning, remind yourself:

This pause is not about doing less.
It is about noticing what my body has been trained to prioritize.

You are invited to notice whether what feels unsafe is actual risk, or the discomfort of interrupting a familiar protection.

Bring to mind a moment from your day when:

- you felt pressure to respond quickly
- you pushed yourself to continue despite fatigue
- you moved ahead without checking capacity (yours or others')
- you felt impatient with delay, confusion, or slowness

This moment may be a work interaction, a family exchange, a meeting, news you consumed, or any other task you rushed through You do not need to analyze it. Simply let the moment return.

Name the moment: ____

The Practice

1 *Pause the Motion*

Stop whatever you are doing for a brief moment. Let your body come to stillness, even slightly. Notice where your weight is supported.

____
____
____
____
____
____

2 *Sense the Body's Response to Stopping*

As you pause, notice agitation, relief, guilt, irritation, fear of falling behind, a pull to resume, or something else. Where does this show up in your body? Stay with one sensation.

____
____
____
____
____
____
____
____
____

3 *Name the Urgency*

Silently ask: *What is the urgency asking me to protect?* You are not looking for a correct answer. Let a phrase, image, or sensation emerge.

4 *Widen the Lens*

Now ask gently: *Who benefits when I do not pause here? Who carries the cost when I continue at this pace?* Let this question land in the body, not the mind.

5 *Choose a Small Interruption*

Without changing the situation dramatically, choose one small act of interruption: one slower breath, one delayed response, one boundary, one moment of acknowledgment, one redistribution of time, attention, or labor onto some other activity that calls to you.

Notice what happens in your body as you choose differently. Notice whether this interruption costs you something, or whether it is already supported by your position.

6 *Close the Practice*

Place a hand somewhere grounding.

Silently say: *I can slow down without abandoning responsibility. I can resist urgency without collapsing.*

Reflection Prompts

(*You may choose one or more, or none at all.*)

- What does my body do when I interrupt momentum, even briefly?
- How is my relationship to speed shaped by caste, class, gender, ability, or role?
- What kind of discomfort shows up when I do not move ahead automatically?
- How might pausing become a relational act rather than an individual choice?

In Friction with Privilege, resistance does not begin with action. It begins with interrupting what feels normal. The pause becomes resistance when it exposes the bodily habits that keep unequal systems running smoothly. Each moment of slowing trains the body to stay present at the edge of discomfort, where accountability becomes possible but not complete.

Lived Experience: Anand

Anand was part of a small group of friends who met every few weeks in the evenings. They were connected through long histories—college friendships, shared political interests, and years of showing up for each other through work stress, caregiving, illness, and transitions. The group had begun experimenting with short collective practices, not as a formal circle, but as a way to slow down how they were with each other.

During one gathering, someone suggested they try the Pause that Disrupts Power practice together. They agreed it would be brief and optional. No one was required to share. As they sat in a loose circle, Anand noticed his body was already restless. Even here, among friends, he felt the familiar pull to stay alert, useful, responsive. When the pause began, he felt irritation rise almost immediately—an urge to check his phone, to move the conversation along, to not "waste time." As the group stayed quiet, Anand felt tightness in his jaw and chest. The thought came quickly: *If I slow down, things will pile up*. He recognized this feeling. It was the same urgency that shaped his days—answering messages quickly, making decisions fast, carrying responsibility without stopping.

What shifted in the group setting was that he did not have to resolve this alone.

After the pause, one friend shared noticing guilt when resting. Another spoke about how speed was rewarded in their family growing up. Hearing this, Anand realized that his urgency was not just personal drive. It was shaped by class, gender, and professional positioning—by being someone whose speed was accommodated by others adjusting around him.

Later, when the group was invited to reflect silently on who enables their ability to pause, Anand pictured interns at work, service workers, family members who waited, friends who absorbed delays. The pause began to feel heavier, but also clearer.

No one asked him to act differently that night. No one demanded a plan. But the next time they met, Anand noticed himself interrupting less. He left more space before responding. When someone suggested slowing the conversation, he did not resist it. The pause had become a shared reference point—something the group could return to together.

Over time, Anand understood the practice not as self-improvement, but as relational accountability. The pause did not dismantle systems of power. Practiced collectively, however, it disrupted his automatic alignment with speed and entitlement. It allowed resistance to move through his body not as guilt or self-critique, but as responsibility held in relationship.

Summary

In the practices offered in this chapter, Friction with Privilege has been approached as both an internal and a relational tension. The body notices discomfort, hesitation, defensiveness, or urgency when privilege became visible. These sensations are not treated as failure, but as information. They show where the body is beginning to sense its location within systems of power, even if meaning had not yet settled.

Calling the Bluff of Privilege begins where friction does not end. It moves from noticing discomfort to examining what that discomfort protects. While friction asks, *What is happening in my body as awareness grows?*, calling the bluff asks, *What story of innocence, neutrality, or inevitability is being upheld so that nothing has to change?*

This shift matters because awareness alone does not disrupt power. Privilege often survives awareness by adapting. It learns to feel bad without changing behavior, to acknowledge injustice without giving up advantage, to speak the language of care while maintaining comfort. The body may continue to tense, explain, or withdraw, but the system remains intact. Calling the Bluff of Privilege is the moment when the body begins to recognize this pattern and refuses to cooperate with it. The next chapter introduced practices to call/name the bluff of privilege and center liberatory hopes of the bodymind and community.

Where does "*Friction with Privilege*" make itself known in your life? Draw or write your reflections in this space...

Chapter 9

Calling the Bluff of Privilege

Calling the Bluff of Privilege refers to the body's recognition that dominant systems rely on certain unspoken assumptions to remain unquestioned. These include beliefs such as: "this is just how things are," "I didn't intend harm," "I am doing my best," or "this issue is too complex for me to act on." These narratives allow privilege to appear reasonable, fragile, or unavoidable, even as harm continues.

In bodily terms, Calling the Bluff of Privilege happens when the familiar strategies of avoidance no longer settle the nervous system. Explanation does not bring relief. Guilt does not discharge. Silence does not feel neutral anymore. The body begins to sense that something is being asked of it that cannot be resolved through internal reflection alone.

Unlike protest, which names the body's response to oppression, Calling the Bluff of Privilege names the moment when a body shaped by relative safety, access, or insulation begins to see how it has benefited from systems that injure others. This recognition is rarely dramatic. More often, it arrives through small ruptures in everyday life: a pause that feels dishonest; a boundary that is never set; a harm that is minimized; a pattern that repeats despite good intentions.

Calling the Bluff of Privilege does not mean becoming morally pure or perfectly accountable. It means noticing where privilege claims helplessness while exercising power, claims ignorance while benefiting from structure, or claims care while avoiding cost. The practices in this chapter invite the body to stay with that recognition long enough for responsibility to become possible. Recognition alone does not undo harm, but it can create the conditions where responsibility can no longer be deferred.

Practice Invitation 1: Testing the Limits of Innocence and Intention

You may take 15–25 minutes for this practice.

This practice supports the body in noticing how claims of *good intention, not knowing*, or *meant well* often function as shields that protect privilege from accountability. In systems shaped by caste, race, class, gender, ability, and neurotypical norms, innocence is not neutral. It is often unevenly distributed and bodily defended. Some bodies are granted the benefit of doubt, while others are required to prove harm repeatedly.

Calling the Bluff of Privilege begins when the body notices how quickly it reaches for innocence in moments of challenge. This practice helps you stay with that reflex; not to

DOI: 10.4324/9781003672203-13

shame it, but to understand what it is protecting and what it costs others. This is a practice of resistance because it interrupts the automatic alignment between intention and impact. It asks the body to remain present when innocence no longer holds.

Choose a setting where you can sit, stand, or move gently without interruption.

Have a notebook nearby if writing feels supportive, though it is not required.

Before beginning, check your capacity. Notice whether "not ready" is about protection from overwhelm, or protection from responsibility. If your body feels flooded, numb, or defensive already, you may return to a grounding practice and come back later.

Remind yourself quietly: *This practice is about awareness, not self-punishment.*

The Practice

Bring to mind a recent moment where your intention felt good, neutral, or reasonable, but where someone else may have been affected differently.

This could include:

- Being corrected about caste language, pronouns, or access needs
- Hearing feedback about exclusion or bias
- Reading or watching news about trans rights, reservation, disability access, labor exploitation, or institutional violence
- A moment when someone named harm and your body responded quickly with explanation, justification, or withdrawal

You are not looking for a dramatic incident.
Everyday moments are enough.

Name the situation: ____

As you recall the situation, notice what happens in your body.

You may sense:

- Tightness in the chest or jaw
- Heat, urgency, or restlessness
- A pull to explain, clarify, or disengage
- A flattening or distancing

Choose one sensation and stay with it.

Name the sensation: ____

Then gently ask the body:

- *What does my innocence want to protect right now?*
- *What feels at risk if I let go of being "well-intentioned"?*

Do not rush for answers.
Let sensations, images, or fragments arise.

If it feels possible, ask one more question:

- *Who has to bear the cost when I ask for my intention to matter more than my impact?*
- *What has allowed me not to notice this cost until now?*

Notice what shifts.
The body may resist. That resistance is part of the practice.

Stay for a few breaths longer than is comfortable, but not until it is overwhelming.

Closing the Practice

Let go of the inquiry gently.

Place a hand somewhere grounding.
Take one slow exhale.

You may write or speak one sentence that captures what you noticed, for example:

- *My body rushes to explain when caste is named.*
- *I protect being "kind" even when harm is pointed out.*

There is no need to resolve anything yet. But something may no longer be unknowable.

Reflection Prompts

If you wish to spend more time with this practice, consider journaling on one or more of the following questions:

- Where does my body reach for innocence most quickly?
- What does letting go of innocence make possible that intention cannot?
- How does my social location shape when I am allowed not to know?
- What might accountability feel like in the body, not just the mind?

Lived Experience: Ayaan

Ayaan, a cis, upper-caste man working in a university setting, prided himself on being progressive. During a team meeting, a Dalit colleague named how decision-making often happened informally, excluding those not part of dominant networks. Ayaan felt an immediate tightening in his throat and a surge of thoughts: *That wasn't my intention. I didn't mean it that way.*

Later, as he practiced Testing the Limits of Innocence and Intention, he stayed with the tightness instead of rehearsing his defense. When he asked what his innocence was protecting, the answer surprised him: *Your image as fair.*

Sitting with that discomfort, he realized how often intention had allowed him to exit accountability. The practice did not tell him what to do next, but it made something undeniable. His body could no longer confuse being well-meaning with being just.

That recognition marked the beginning of resistance, not against others, but against the habits that kept power intact.

Practice Invitation 2: Redistributing Small Costs

Privilege often operates by concentrating comfort and dispersing cost. Some bodies absorb exhaustion, risk, silencing, or adjustment so that others can remain uninterrupted.

This practice invites you to notice where your body is accustomed to ease, efficiency, or protection, and to experiment with redistributing *small, everyday costs* rather than avoiding them.

Calling the Bluff of Privilege does not require grand gestures. It does require that some ease actually shifts. It begins when the body learns to tolerate inconvenience, discomfort, or loss of ease in service of shared dignity. This is a practice of resistance because it interrupts the silent agreements that keep harm outsourced.

You may take 10–20 minutes for reflection, followed by lived experimentation over a day or week.

Choose a moment when your body feels reasonably steady.

Remind yourself: *This practice is about responsibility, not heroism.*

The Practice

Begin by noticing where your life currently feels smooth, efficient, or uninterrupted. Then bring to mind one everyday context, such as:

- Workspaces or meetings
- Family routines
- Public spaces
- Activist or "progressive" circles
- Food, language, timing, pace, access

Name the context: ____

Ask yourself:

- *Where do others adjust so I don't have to?*
- *Where is my comfort made possible by someone else's silence, labor, or flexibility?*

Let your body respond before you decide anything.

Notice sensations such as:

- Hesitation
- Tightening
- Fatigue
- Relief at the thought of not opting out

____
____
____
____
____
____

Now choose one small cost you could absorb instead of passing it on. Notice whether this cost feels meaningful to your body, or merely acceptable.

This might look like:

- Slowing your pace in a neurodivergent-friendly space
- Asking rather than assuming access needs
- Staying present in conversations about caste or trans rights instead of changing the subject
- Taking feedback without immediate response
- Giving up convenience, recognition, or control in a small way

Name the cost: ____

Ask the body: *What does it feel like to carry this cost myself?*

____
____
____
____
____
____

Stay with the sensation.

Closing the Practice

You may name one small, concrete action you are willing to take or repeat.

Let it be modest.
Let it be ongoing.
Let it be noticeable to you

Take one breath to mark the commitment.

Reflection Prompts

Choose one or more of the following questions to journal about.

- What costs have I been protected from noticing?
- Which discomforts feel "too much," and what does that reveal about my position?
- How does my body react when I choose inconvenience over ease?
- What changes when responsibility is shared rather than explained away?

Lived Experience: Meera

Meera, a cis, upper-caste woman, is part of a queer collective that meets regularly to plan events, share resources, and support one another. The group prides itself on being caring and politically conscious. Meetings are lively, ideas move quickly, and decisions are often made late into the night. Meera has always experienced this pace as energizing. It feels like commitment, like being alive together.

During a collective session where the group explored redistributing small costs, the facilitator invited everyone to reflect on a recent gathering and notice where effort, endurance, or accommodation might have been unevenly held. As others shared, Meera felt a subtle restlessness in her legs and a tightness behind her eyes. She wanted to move on, to solve something, to keep the energy going.

When she stayed with the sensation, an uncomfortable realization surfaced. She began to notice how some neurodivergent members often went quiet as meetings stretched on, turning cameras off or withdrawing into themselves. No one named this directly. The group simply kept moving. The cost of overstimulation was being absorbed silently so the collective could maintain speed.

In the group discussion that followed, Meera spoke about her discomfort. She named how slowing down felt threatening to her, as if momentum itself was a sign of care and seriousness. Hearing herself say it out loud, she recognized how efficiency had become a moral value in her body. Being able to tolerate intensity was something she had always assumed was neutral, even generous. The group helped her see that it was also shaped by privilege, by a body that was less likely to be overwhelmed by pace and noise.

Nothing was resolved in that session. No one redesigned the collective overnight. But something shifted in how Meera listened.

At the next meeting, when the agenda began to stretch and voices piled on, Meera noticed the familiar restlessness return. This time, she recognized it as a signal. Instead of pushing through it, she suggested a short pause and asked whether the pace was working for everyone. Her voice felt exposed. The suggestion landed unevenly. Some people welcomed it. Others were quiet.

Later, a few members thanked her privately and said the pause had helped them stay present.

For Meera, this was not about becoming "better" or more aware in theory. It was about learning to carry a small cost herself, the discomfort of slowing down and interrupting familiar rhythms, rather than letting that cost be absorbed by others. Resistance, she realized, was not loud or dramatic. It was the practice of letting ease redistribute, even when it unsettled her own sense of what felt right.

Practice Invitation 3: Compassionate Repair and Reconnection

This practice supports the movement from bodily awareness into relational accountability. It is for moments when privilege has already been noticed and can no longer be unseen, and the question becomes not "Did I mean harm?" but "What does responsibility require now?"

Calling the Bluff of Privilege means refusing the comfort of innocence. It asks the body to stay present when repair is needed, even when returning feels awkward, risky, or destabilizing. This practice does not aim to resolve harm neatly or quickly. It also does not aim to restore comfort for the person holding power. Instead, it supports the body in learning how to return, listen, and remain in relationship without collapsing into guilt or defensiveness.

Repair here is understood as a form of resistance. It interrupts the pattern where privilege absorbs harm and moves on untouched. Each act of repair redistributes a small cost back to the body that holds power, allowing accountability to become lived rather than abstract.

Choose one situation where you sense unresolved tension linked to privilege. This might be interpersonal, institutional, or internal.

Examples include:

- A moment where you spoke over someone and later recognized how caste, race, class, gender, or professional authority shaped that interaction.
- A silence you maintained when a trans or disabled person was misrepresented or erased.
- A decision that benefited you but placed strain or invisibility on others.
- A discomfort you moved past quickly without staying with its implications.

Name the situation: ____

Ensure you feel resourced enough to reflect. If your body feels overwhelmed, orient first to the room, the ground beneath you, or something steady nearby. This practice can be returned to later or done alongside someone who can witness without rescuing.

Place one hand on a part of your body that feels warm or solid. Take a few slow breaths.

You may silently say: *I am not here to defend myself. I am here to return.*

Let this be an orientation rather than a demand.

The Practice

Bring the unresolved moment to mind, not as a story to analyze but as an experience the body remembers. Notice where the body responds first. It might be a tightening in the chest, a drop in the stomach, heat in the face, or a heaviness in the shoulders.

Name where the body responds: ______________________________________

Stay with one sensation.

Without judging it, ask:

- *What did I move past too quickly?*
- *What did my body know then that I did not stay with?*

____
____
____
____
____
____

Allow any emotions to be present. Sadness, fear, embarrassment, regret, or confusion may arise. These are not problems to solve but signals that something meaningful is at stake.

Then ask:

- *What do I wish I had been able to hear or see in that moment?*
- *What way of being do I want my body to practice now?*

Let the answer be simple and specific. It may sound like:

- "I want to listen without explaining."
- "I want to name harm without centering myself."
- "I want to slow down instead of moving on."

____
____
____
____
____
____

If it feels appropriate, shape this into a small declaration of repair. Not a promise of perfection, but a direction of practice. For example:

"I am willing to return and listen, even if it is uncomfortable."
"I am practicing staying when my instinct is to withdraw."
"I am learning to let repair take time."

____
____
____
____
____
____

Repair becomes accountable when it costs something familiar.

Finally, place both hands on a grounded surface. Let your body register steadiness. This gesture marks the difference between intention and embodied commitment.

Lived Experience: Shraddha

Shraddha, a neurotypical woman in a long-term relationship with a neurodivergent partner, often described herself as patient and supportive. Yet during moments of sensory overload or shutdown, she found herself irritated, interpreting her partner's withdrawal as indifference.

After a tense argument, Shraddha noticed a familiar pattern: a rush to explain her intentions, followed by emotional distance. In the Compassionate Repair and Reconnection practice, she stayed with the heaviness in her chest and asked what she wished she had understood.

The answer came quietly: *This is not about effort. It's about different nervous systems.*

Instead of rehearsing an apology that centered her frustration, Shraddha practiced sitting with the discomfort of having misread the situation. When she returned to her partner, she said, "*I realized I was expecting you to process the way I do. I want to learn how to meet you where you are.*"

The repair was slow and imperfect. But something shifted. Shraddha's body learned that resistance was not about fixing the relationship quickly. It was about staying present when her assumptions were unsettled. Responsibility became relational, not performative.

Summary

This chapter has approached resistance not as a virtue, identity, or dramatic act, but as a bodily threshold. A place where awareness meets protection, and where the body begins to sense that familiar ways of holding power, comfort, or neutrality are no longer sufficient.

Across the practices of Friction with Privilege and Calling the Bluff of Privilege, resistance has been located not in intention, but in what the body does when dominant arrangements are unsettled. Tightening, urgency, explanation, silence, withdrawal, speed, and collapse have all been treated not as failures, but as meaningful signals. They show where the body has learned to preserve moral ease, relational safety, or exemption from cost.

A central thread running through this chapter is the decentering of moral innocence. Moral innocence refers to the belief, often bodily rather than explicit, that being well-intentioned, caring, or marginalized in some ways should protect one from being implicated in harm. It shows up as the need to be seen as "good," "not like others," or "doing one's best," even when impact has been named. Moral innocence is not a personality trait. It is a structural position that some bodies are more able to inhabit and defend than others.

Decentering moral innocence does not mean replacing it with shame or self-attack. It means loosening the body's dependence on innocence as a shield. It means allowing responsibility to exist without requiring purity, certainty, or exemption. In bodily terms, it is the shift from asking, "Did I mean harm?" to asking, "What is being protected if nothing changes?" and "What is my body being asked to carry now?"

Letting go of moral innocence can widen perception and make it possible to stay present when impact is named. But the loss of innocence, on its own, is not accountability. It simply removes one of the protections that allows harm to continue without interruption.

The distinction this workbook makes between protest and resistance is crucial here. Protest names how marginalized bodies respond to precarity, harm, and ongoing exposure. It is the body's strategy for survival under unequal conditions. Resistance, as used in this chapter, names something different. It names what happens when bodies shaped by relative insulation begin to notice how they have been positioned, what they have not had to endure, and how their comfort has been maintained through systems that harm others.

In this sense, resistance is not automatic. It is learned. It must be practiced. It emerges when friction is not bypassed, when innocence is not defended, and when discomfort is not collapsed into guilt or explanation. It grows through small, repeated acts of staying, redistributing cost, slowing down, repairing, and relinquishing the need to be exempt.

What these practices collectively offer is not a map toward moral correctness, but a reorientation of the body toward shared responsibility. Resistance here is not opposition for its own sake. It is the steady, relational capacity to remain present when power is revealed, to absorb some of the discomfort that has been unevenly distributed, and to allow one's own body to change how it moves through the world.

Seen this way, the Body as a Site of Resistance is not heroic or resolved. It is tentative, learning, and ongoing. It is a body that no longer relies on innocence to stay intact. It is a body willing to be shaped by accountability, relationship, and the slow work of collective liberation. Being shaped by accountability means allowing patterns of comfort, speed, and exemption to change, not just be understood.

When bodies shaped by privilege learn to stay with resistance in this way, something else becomes possible. The body's capacity to sense friction, tolerate the loss of innocence, and redistribute comfort does not only support ethical accountability. It also deepens the ability to recognize protest and to stand alongside liberation without appropriating it.

As resistance is practiced, the body becomes less defended and more responsive. This creates the conditions to perceive protest more clearly—not as threat, accusation, or inconvenience, but as necessary, relational truth arising from precarity. It also strengthens the capacity to engage liberation not as entitlement or performance, but as shared possibility shaped by responsibility.

In this way, Body as a Site of Resistance does not stand apart from Body as a Site of Protest or Body as a Site of Liberation. It prepares the ground for them. Resistance trains the body to relinquish insulation, to remain present in discomfort, and to orient toward collective accountability. From this ground, solidarity becomes possible, dignity becomes relational, and displaying what is our right can emerge without reproducing harm.

As the final part of this workbook, Body as a Site of Resistance does not close the arc so much as widen it. When people learn to stay with friction, question moral innocence, and call the bluff of privilege without collapsing into shame or withdrawal, they often find that earlier capacities deepen rather than disappear. The body becomes more available as a site of protest, able to name harm and refuse erasure without numbing. It also becomes more available as a site of liberation, capable of sensing what is right, possible, and worth moving toward.

> Resistance, in this sense, is not opposed to aliveness or care. It is one of the ways care learns to take responsibility for its impact in the world.

What emerges is not a perfected ethical subject, but a body that can stay in relationship with difficulty, contradiction, and change. This is not the end of the work. It is one way the work stays alive.

How does "*Calling the Bluff of Privilege*" show itself in your body and the way you navigate the world? Draw or write your reflections in this space...

Chapter 10

The Ongoing Practice of Returning

Practices You Have Met Along the Way

Across this workbook, you have encountered a wide range of practices. Some were quiet and subtle. Some were relational. Some invited noticing. Some invited staying. Some invited refusal, withdrawal, or disruption. These practices were not designed as a linear progression or a fixed toolkit. They were offered as ways of meeting different moments, under different conditions, and from different locations of power and vulnerability.

You may remember practices that supported aliveness, such as sensing the pulse of life, noticing what felt pleasant or unpleasant, tracking what mattered, or finding language that asserted your right to exist and to take up space.

You may recall practices that helped you stay with protest, such as grounding while remaining aware of systemic forces; withholding engagement; staying with a clear "no"; or allowing freeze, silence, or non-response to be recognized as meaningful rather than corrected.

You may remember practices that asked you to stay with friction, such as noticing discomfort around privilege, complicity, or innocence; attending to everyday moments where power shows up; redistributing small costs; or pausing in ways that subtly disrupt familiar dynamics.

Some of these practices may still feel alive.
Some may feel distant, irritating, or no longer relevant.
Some may never have fit.

None of these responses mean that the work has failed or been abandoned.

Practices in this workbook were never meant to be carried forward unchanged. They were meant to do their work and then step aside when conditions shifted, when other supports became necessary, or when the body asked for something different.

This chapter does not ask you to choose which practices to keep.

It asks you to notice what has already stayed, what has fallen away, and what has transformed into something else entirely.

DOI: 10.4324/9781003672203-14

A Closing Practice: The Tree Metaphor

Before reading further, you are invited to pause.

Across this workbook the practices can be seen through the metaphor of the tree, as a way of thinking about embodied social justice, not as a structure to master, but as a way of holding together identity, conditions, sensation, and response without forcing them into order (Figure 3).

You may return to the tree here, or you may choose not to.

This is not a review of earlier chapters, and it is not an assessment of what you have learned.

Instead, this is an invitation to notice where you are now, under the conditions you are currently living within.

> You are invited to draw your own tree, or something that does not resemble a tree at all.
> You may use the tree that Aarathi drew, as shown below, as a reference, or set it aside entirely.

> It does not need to be coherent.
> It does not need to be complete.

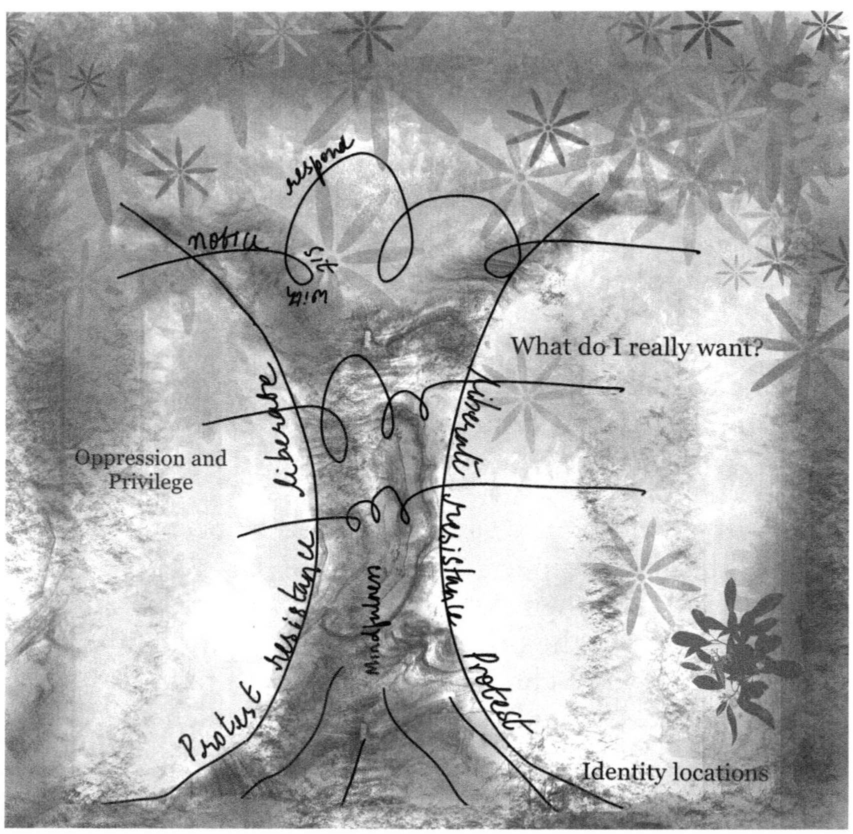

Figure 3 Embodied Tree.

You may draw only parts, or leave large spaces empty.

This practice is not meant to clarify the work or bring it to resolution.

It is meant to make visible what is holding, what is constrained, and what has already shifted, whether or not that shift feels intentional or legible.

You may take a few minutes to draw, write, or mark a page now.
You may also return to this later, or skip it entirely.

What follows in this chapter does not depend on completing this exercise.

It offers a way of thinking about returning that does not rely on continuity, discipline, or progress.

You may let the following questions sit nearby as you draw or write.
You do not need to respond to all of them.

This final chapter is an invitation to pause—to sense the quiet ripple of all that has been learned and unlearned. Through these pages, you have met the Body as a Site of Liberation, a Site of Protest, and a Site Resistance. You have turned toward sensations that once felt unbearable, breathed through the edges of shame or fear, and listened for the wisdom carried in your own pulse.

Integration asks for rhythm, finding a sustainable way to return, again and again, to awareness, compassion, and connection even when life moves fast or fractures return. Mindfulness, in the context of social justice, is not a state we achieve but a relationship we keep cultivating—with our bodies, communities, and the world.

To integrate is to keep noticing how systems live through us, how care must be practiced collectively, and how each act of presence becomes a thread in the wider fabric of justice.

Practice Invitation

Use the space below to draw your tree—however imperfect, however complete, this tree stands testament to the journey you have undertaken in this workbook.

You might draw:

- roots, or just ground
- a trunk, or something holding
- branches, or fractures, or lines moving outward
- nothing that looks like a tree at all

Use words, shapes, arrows, symbols, or marks.
You may leave space. You may cross things out.
There is no correct form.

You may let these questions sit nearby as you draw or write.
You do not need to respond to all of them.

Roots: Identity and Constraint

- What identity locations feel most present right now?
- Which offer protection, privilege, or ease?
- Which carry risk, scrutiny, or cost?
- What feels difficult or unsafe to name?

Conditions: Around the Tree

- What conditions are shaping your movement right now?
- Where do you feel demand, extraction, or pressure?
- Where do you feel buffered or insulated?
- What choices feel unavailable because of these conditions?

What Is Holding (Trunk of the Tree)

- What is holding you right now?
- What are you no longer holding up by effort?
- What has stopped working, even if it once helped?

Where Response Came First (Helix of Notice, Sit With, and Respond)

- Where did your body act before you had words for it?
- Where did having words not change what was possible?

The Question

Instead of asking *What do I really want?*, you might ask:

- What feels unsafe, unavailable, or unrealistic to want right now?

You may leave this unanswered.

ONE SMALL SHIFT, ALREADY OCCURRED

Without planning or committing:

- Has anything changed in where you go, what you tolerate, or what you refuse?
- Has something become less available, or easier, because something else stopped?

If you choose, write these shifts within the leaves of your tree.

My Tree, My Journey…

Closing

You do not need to complete this tree.
You may return to it, redraw it, or never look at it again.
Returning does not always mean coming back inward.
Sometimes it means noticing when the work has moved elsewhere.

The Ongoing Practice of Returning

This final chapter is not an ending. It is an invitation to stay in relationship with what you have already encountered, without turning that relationship into a task, a responsibility, or a measure of progress.

Across this workbook, you have met the Body as a Site of Liberation, a Site of Protest, and a Site of Resistance. You have noticed moments of aliveness and expansion. You have stayed with refusal, freeze, silence, and withdrawal without forcing movement. You have encountered friction, especially where comfort, privilege, or familiarity were unsettled. None of these experiences were meant to resolve into clarity or certainty. They were meant to be met.

What follows is not guidance on how to continue practicing. It is an orientation toward how returning happens, again and again, in ways that are shaped by capacity, context, and conditions rather than intention alone.

Returning is Not Regression

There may be times when what felt accessible earlier no longer feels possible. Sensation may become faint, confusing, overwhelming, or distant. Practices that once felt supportive may now feel irritating, irrelevant, or too demanding. You may notice yourself avoiding certain chapters, certain kinds of inquiry, or the workbook itself.

This is not a sign that something has been lost.

Bodies change with context. Risk shifts. Energy fluctuates. What the body is responding to now may be very different from what it was responding to when you first began. A return to stillness may feel impossible because stillness is no longer safe. A return to inquiry may feel distant because the body is busy protecting something essential. A return to reflection may feel unnecessary because the body already knows what it needs to do.

Returning does not mean going back to the beginning or repeating earlier steps. It means recognizing when the body is asking for distance, when it is asking for support, and when it is asking to be left alone. These movements are not interruptions to the work. They are expressions of it.

In this framework, returning is not linear. It does not follow improvement or decline. It follows conditions.

Rhythm Instead of Discipline

In many mindfulness traditions, continuation is framed as consistency. Daily practice. Commitment. Maintenance. These ideas may land similar to the logic from productivity and self-regulation, even when they are offered gently. This workbook does not ask for discipline in that sense.

What it offers instead is rhythm. Rhythm shaped by pain cycles, by caregiving, by sensory load, by collective responsibilities, by grief, by political moments, by exhaustion, by joy.

Rhythm that changes over time.

There may be periods when returning looks like regular engagement with a particular practice. There may be long stretches when returning looks like remembering one sentence, one sensation, or one moment of refusal. There may be times when returning does not involve this workbook at all; rather, it shows up in how you pace yourself in a conversation, how you stop speaking sooner than expected, how you take rest without justification, or how you notice your body withdrawing and decide not to override it.

Returning does not require effort every time. Sometimes it arrives as recognition. Sometimes it arrives as relief. Sometimes it arrives as irritation. All of these are ways the body stays in relationship.

From Practices to Conditions of Care

As you move away from the structured practices in this workbook, it becomes important to notice what actually makes embodied awareness possible—not practices, but conditions.

Conditions such as having enough time to slow down without penalty. Conditions such as being in spaces where silence is not immediately interpreted or filled. Conditions such as having your boundaries respected without explanation, being able to move, stim, rest, or disengage without being corrected. Conditions such as practicing alongside others who share the site of protest or friction you are working with. Conditions such as material support, reduced exposure to harm, and access to accompaniment.

Without these conditions, returning becomes harder, no matter how skilled or committed someone is. This is not a personal limitation. It is a political reality.

Embodied social justice does not ask individuals to carry the cost of injustice more skillfully. It asks us to notice where care must be redistributed, where expectations must be reduced, and where collective responsibility must replace individual endurance. Returning, then, is also about noticing when the conditions are not present and letting that be named without self-blame.

Collective Holding and Shared Return

Although many of the practices within this workbook can be engaged with alone, the work it points toward is not meant to be carried in isolation. Bodies learn what is possible through relationship. Protest becomes clearer when it is recognized. Resistance becomes sustainable when it is shared. Liberation becomes imaginable when it is witnessed.

This does not mean everyone needs a group, a community, or a formal space. Collective holding can take many forms. It may look like practicing alongside one other person without processing. It may look like a space where silence is protected. It may look like a relationship where your withdrawal is not questioned. It may look like a pause that is honored rather than filled.

It also means recognizing when certain spaces are not appropriate for this work. Not every group, workplace, classroom, or community setting can hold protest or friction safely. Choosing not to bring this work into those spaces is not avoidance. It is discernment.

Returning in collective ways is not about visibility or sharing. It is about not being alone with what the body already knows.

Take a minute to explore "*What does collective holding look like in your space?*"

Staying Without Closure

There is no point at which this work is completed.

The body will continue to respond to the world. Systems will continue to press, protect, extract, and offer uneven access to safety and dignity. Sensation will continue to signal when something is too much, when something is misaligned, when something wants to move, and when something wants to stop.

You may return to this workbook many times. You may also set it aside and never open it again. Neither choice determines the depth of your engagement with embodied social justice.

What matters is not continuity, but permission.

Permission to pause.
Permission to return.
Permission to refuse.
Permission to adapt.
Permission to let the work shape itself around the body rather than asking the body to shape itself around the work.

Returning, in this sense, is not a promise. It is an opening.

Whenever the conditions allow, your body already knows how to find its way back.

Lived Experience: A Shared Return

A few months after finishing the workbook, five people met in a small online group. There was no agenda and no facilitator. They had agreed to check in once, to see what had stayed with them and what had not.

Some had brought notebooks. Others came empty-handed.

For a while, no one spoke.

Then one person said,

I realized something uncomfortable. I was doing the practices, writing, noticing, tracking my body. And I could feel myself becoming more articulate about injustice without actually changing how I lived. I was still protected by the same caste and class buffers. The workbook didn't cause that. But it didn't interrupt it either.

No one rushed to respond.

Another person said,

For me, it was the opposite. I couldn't really do the reflection parts. I skipped most of the writing. But something shifted in how I stopped forcing myself in conversations. I started leaving earlier without explaining. In spaces where I'm usually expected to perform gratitude or compliance, I just didn't. That felt like protest. Quiet, but real.

Someone else hesitated before speaking. "*I struggled with the focus on sensation. Not because it was wrong. But because my body has been watched, corrected, and medicalized for most of my life. Turning inward felt like more surveillance*". They paused. *What helped instead was changing where I went and how long I stayed. I stopped attending meetings where my body was treated as an example. I took routes that felt less exposed. I didn't process what happened. I just didn't go back. That was the action. My body settled after that, not before.*

No one reframed what they had said.

Another person spoke next. "*I think what stayed with me was the permission to stop. But I'm uneasy about that. I could see how easily 'respecting capacity' could slide into protecting comfort.*" They took a breath.
I had to keep asking myself which pauses were care, and which were only possible because I'm insulated. For me, action looked like not opting out when I could have. I stayed in a conversation I usually leave by becoming reflective or tired. I didn't explain myself well. I didn't soften it. I didn't leave feeling good. But something shifted in how the space worked afterward.

Someone else nodded.

That question landed very differently depending on where we sit. Some of us pause because the cost of engagement is already too high. Some of us pause because the cost has never really reached us. I don't think those pauses mean the same thing.

The group sat with that.

One person said, "*I appreciated the gentleness of the language. I needed it. But there were moments when I wanted something firmer. Not kinder, but clearer. Something that named loss. Not just discomfort, but what I might actually have to give up*". They continued, *Action, for me, meant letting the cost reach me a little. I said no to an opportunity that would have kept me comfortable and visible. I lost access to a space where I was praised but not accountable. I didn't repair a rupture just to feel settled again.*

Another person said quietly, "*I don't know if a workbook can do that. Or if that only happens in relationships where someone else bears the cost if we don't move.*"

Someone laughed softly. "*Maybe that's the point. Maybe the workbook isn't the work. Maybe it only points to where the work refuses to stay individual.*"

Another added,

I don't really use the workbook anymore. But I changed how I work. I stopped taking on roles where I was protected and affirmed but not accountable. I refer out more. I earn less some months. I don't call that integration. I just know my body isn't bracing in the same way.

No one tried to decide what that meant.

They talked about places where the practices had felt supportive. They talked about places where they had felt irrelevant, irritating, or too slow. They named moments where the language helped them stay with refusal, and moments where it made it too easy to stay inside their own experience.

At one point, someone said, "*I think what matters is not whether this workbook works for everyone, but whether it lets us be honest about when it doesn't—especially across caste, disability, and class.*"

There was a long silence after that.

Before leaving, one person said, "*I don't think returning means coming back to these pages. I think it means staying in conversation with the questions, especially the ones that don't settle.*"

No one disagreed.

They logged off without conclusions.

Concluding Thoughts

What this conversation makes visible is not a set of answers, but a way of staying. Staying with tension. Staying with disagreement. Staying with the unevenness of cost, capacity, and consequence. The work of embodied social justice does not resolve into agreement or coherence. It continues through dialogue, refusal, missteps, and return.

This workbook does not offer a final position to arrive at. It offers a way of noticing when the work has moved beyond these pages and when it has asked to be argued with instead. Returning, in this sense, is not about loyalty to a practice or a framework. It is about remaining in relationship with what justice asks of the body now, in this moment, under these conditions. Wherever that relationship takes you next.

It will not look the same for everyone.
And it will not always be recognizable as this work.
That, too, is part of returning.

Recommended Resources

This is a curated list of resources to support and accompany the workbook. It is not intended to be exhaustive or definitive. Rather, it is offered as a springboard for further exploration, learning, and engagement with ideas, practices, and scholarship that inform the work of embodied social justice.

Books

1. **Annihilation of Caste**—B.R. Ambedkar
2. **My Grandmother's Hands: Racialized Trauma and the Pathway to Mending Our Hearts and Bodies**—Resmaa Menakem
3. **The Inner Work of Racial Justice: Healing Ourselves and Transforming Our Communities through Mindfulness**—Rhonda V. Magee
4. **Trauma of Caste: A Dalit Feminist Meditation on Survivorship, Healing, and Abolition**—Thenmozhi Soundararajan
5. **The Politics of Trauma**—Staci K. Haines
6. **Embodied Social Justice**—Rae Johnson
7. **McMindfulness: How Mindfulness Became the New Capitalist Spirituality**—Ronald E. Purser
8. **Unraveling Assumptions: A Primer for Understanding Oppression and Privilege**—Karen L. Suyemoto, Roxanne A. Donovan, and Grace S. Kim
9. **Fumbling Toward Repair: A Workbook for Community Accountability Facilitators**—Shira Hassan and Mariame Kaba
10. **Creative Interventions Toolkit: A Practical Guide to Stop Interpersonal Violence**—Creative Interventions (collective)
11. **Black Liturgies: Prayers, Poems, and Meditations for Staying Human**—Cole Arthur Riley
12. **Meet the Savarnas: Indian Millennials Whose Mediocrity Broke Everything**—Ravikant Kisan
13. **Queer Affirmative Counselling Practice: A Resource Book for Mental Health Practitioners in India**—Ketki Ranade, Shruti Chakravarty, Pooja Nair, and Gauri Shringarpure

DOI: 10.4324/9781003672203-15

Picture Books

1. **Leo and the Octopus**—Isabelle Marinov and Chris Nixon
2. **The Boy in the Cupboard**—Harshala Gupte and Priya Dali
3. **Jamlo Walks**—Samina Mishra and Tarique Aziz
4. **I Talk Like a River**—Jordan Scott and Sydney Smith
5. **Guthli Has Wings**—Kanak Shashi
6. **Julian Is a Mermaid**—Jessica Love
7. **The Heart and the Bottle**—Oliver Jeffers
8. **The Gender Wheel: A Story About Bodies and Gender for Everybody**—Maya Gonzalez
9. **The Hero, Babasaheb**—Priyanka Patil
10. **Ish**—Peter H. Reynolds
11. **Cicada**—Shaun Tan

Instagram (Creators/Pages)

Body and Social Justice

- **Ailey Jolie**—@aileyjolie (mindfulness, embodiment, social justice)
- **Mangesh Daliwale** @mangesh.dahiwale (Anticaste Ambedkarite Buddhist)

Organizations (India)

- @pauseforperspective **Pause for Perspective**—Hyderabad-based mental health organization
- @Pauselibrary **Pause Library**
- @npicollective **Narrative Practices India** (**NPI**)—Narrative therapy training collective in India
- @champacabooks **Bookstore**

Anti-Caste Scholars/Writers (Papers & Websites)

1. **Shireen Azam**—Dalit feminist scholar and researcher
   https://scholar.google.com/citations?user=McHilS4AAAAJ&hl=en
2. **Christina Dhanuja**—Scholar and practitioner working at the intersection of caste, gender, and mental health
   https://christinadhanuja.com/elementor-128/
3. **Sushrut Jadhav**—Medical anthropologist, SOAS University of London
   https://www.soas.ac.uk/about/sushrut-jadhav

Disability Justice & Mad Studies

1. **Neuroqueer Heresies: Notes on the Neurodiversity Paradigm**—Nick Walker
2. **We're All Neurodiverse: How to Build a Neurodiversity-Affirming Future and Challenge Neuronormativity**—Sonny Jane Wise

3. **Beyond Survival: Strategies and Stories from the Transformative Justice Movement**—Ejeris Dixon and Leah Lakshmi Piepzna-Samarasinha
4. **Disability Visibility: First-Person Stories from the Twenty-First Century**—Alice Wong (editor)
5. **The Routledge International Handbook of Mad Studies**—Peter Beresford and Jasna Russo (editors)
6. **Contours of Ableism: The Production of Disability and Abledness**—Fiona Kumari Campbell

Poems

1. **Wild Geese**—Mary Oliver
2. **The Guest House**—Rumi (Jalāl ad-Dīn Rūmī)
3. **Kindness**—Naomi Shihab Nye
4. **Hope Is a Sewer Rat**—Caitlin Seida
5. **I am Not Your Data**—Abhay Xaxa
6. **(Works by) G.N. Saibaba**—Indian activist and poet
7. **(Works by) John O'Donohue**—Irish poet and philosopher
8. **Everything Is Waiting for You**—David Whyte
9. **Letters to a Young Poet**—Rainer Maria Rilke

Appendix A

Mapping Your Body's Sensations

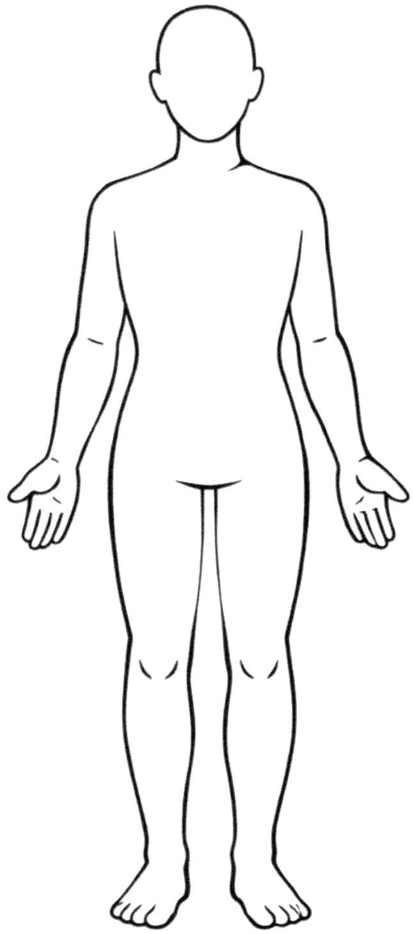

Draw and Name
Your Body's Sensation

____

____

____

____

____

____

Figure 4 Body Outline.

Appendix B

Body Mapping Exercise

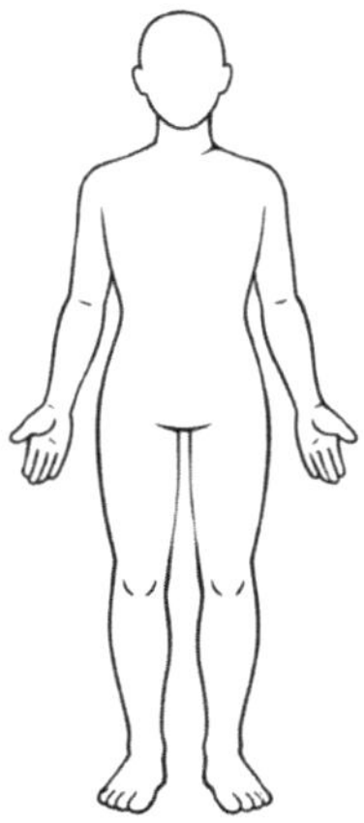

When my body begins to protect me, I usually feel:

This often happens when:

This reveals something about the environment, relationship, or situation, namely that:

What do I really want for myself and those that I care:

What may be that one or more things that is already in motion towards this hope:

Figure 5 Body Mapping Exercise.

Appendix C

Letters as a Practice of Relationship and Accountability

One way to engage with the Five Relational Orientations of Change is through letter-writing. These letters are not a technique, reflection exercise, or form of self-improvement. They are a way of noticing how bodies relate within the conditions of their lives.

Many of us were taught to locate difficulty inside ourselves. Because of this, beginning with Body, Emotions, Sensations, and Thoughts (BEST) can help create contact without urgency, fixing, or analysis. BEST is offered here as an entry point, not as the center of this practice.

Staying only with BEST risks turning systemic harm into personal work. This practice, therefore, asks for a deliberate shift: from the body as a starting place, to context as the center, with accountability as non-optional.

Step One: BEST as an Entry Point (Not the Destination)

You may begin by writing to:

- Your Body
- Your Emotions
- Your Sensations
- Your Thoughts

using one of the Five Relational Orientations of Change.

- Remembering Finiteness
- Generosity as Movement, Not Obligation
- Living Boundaries
- Nourishing Intake
- Words as Connection

You may write one line.
You may write nothing.
Reading quietly counts.

Figure 6a Living Boundaries.

BEST is used here to slow down and orient to experience.
It is not used to regulate, discipline, or improve the self.
If your writing begins to sound like self-correction, self-management, or self-blame, pause.

That is information.

Figure 6a offers some examples of letter-writing using BEST. We offer this as a visual prompt to start your own writing. Your letters may be longer, shorter, more poetic. Allow your voice to flow unfiltered.

Step Two: Shifting the Center to Context

Not everything that tightens, numbs, exhausts, or silences you originates within your body.

After beginning with BEST, you are invited to shift the letter away from the self and toward context.

You may write to:

- Caste
- Race
- Respectability
- Purity
- Ableist time
- Cis-heteronormativity
- Family scripts
- Institutions
- Work cultures
- Access barriers
- Safety
- Silence
- Privilege
- Or something else: ______________________________

This shift matters.

It helps keep harm located where it belongs, rather than asking the body to carry what is structural. You do not need to explain, analyze, or resolve what you name. Noticing is enough.

The following example (Figure 6b) is just *one* way a letter might look when the focus shifts away from the self and toward context.

It is not meant to be copied or completed.

Dear Ableist Time,

You move *fast* and pretend it is neutral.

You reward bodies that can keep up
and quietly punish those that cannot.

You taught me that slowing down needs justification.
That fatigue is a personal failure.

That asking for more time is asking for too much.

Today, I am noticing how often ***my body tightens*** around you.
How my ***breath*** shortens when I try to meet your pace.

I am **not** trying to change you here.

I am **naming** you so my body does no thave to carry you alone.

Figure 6b Dear Ableist Time.

Step Three: Accountability (This Does Not Land the Same for Everyone)

Please read the section that fits your current location.

If you are marginalized in the situation you are writing about, you are not required to:

- Make meaning
- Heal
- Forgive
- Continue writing

Silence, refusal, shutdown, withdrawal, or stopping are all legitimate responses.

You may choose to end the worksheet here.

- I am stopping here
- I want to underline one line instead
- I want to rest

If you are socially privileged in the situation you are writing about, accountability cannot remain internal. For you, this practice is not about awareness alone. It is about responsibility. You are invited to write letters that clarify:

- what I benefit from
- what I will no longer take
- what I will interrupt
- what I will redistribute
- what I am willing to lose

These letters are not confessions.
They are not apologies.
They are not requests for absolution.
Embodied awareness without material change is not accountability.

The following example (Figure 6c) is offered to show how accountability might appear in writing. It is not an instruction or a measure of adequacy.

Writing Your Own Letters

If it feels supportive, you are invited to write your own letters using:

- One relational orientation
- One element of BEST or
- A letter addressed directly to context

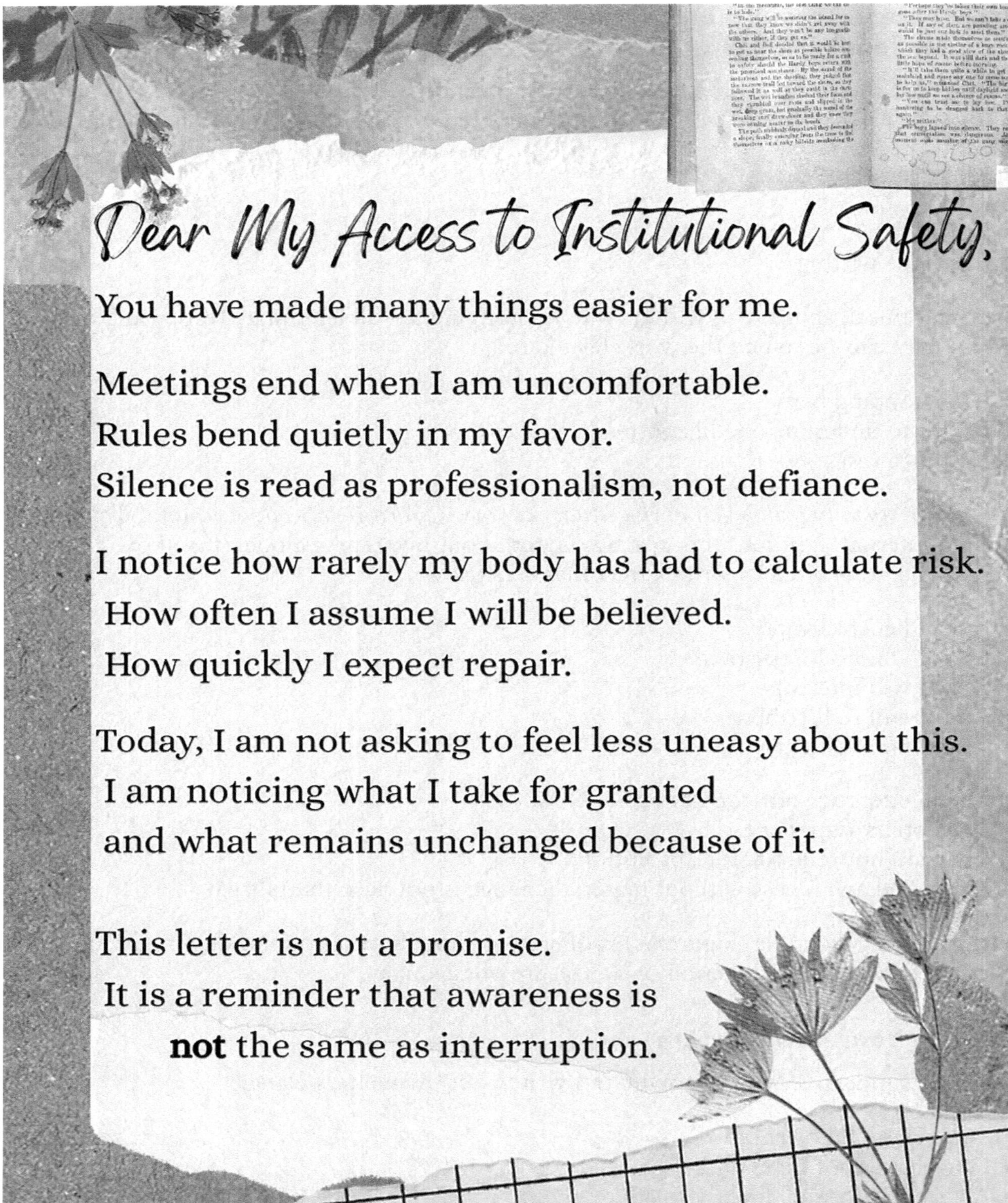

Figure 6c Dear My Access to Institutional Safety.

You may write:

- A single line
- A fragment
- An unfinished note

You may also choose not to write.
Writing is optional.
Stopping is part of the practice.

Ways to Engage without Writing

You may instead:

- Underline one phrase that feels true
- Notice one sensation without naming it
- Name one condition shaping your body
- Pause and stop

There is no requirement to complete anything.

If This Is Done in a Group

If sharing feels appropriate, people may share:

- A sensation
- A metaphor
- A single line

Stories are not required.
Witnessing is not owed.

A Closing Orientation

These letters are not meant to make you better.

They are meant to help you notice how bodies respond to power, care, risk, and possibility.

BEST helps you begin.
Context keeps the work honest.
Accountability keeps the practice ethical.
Change is constant.
Care is negotiated.
Your body already knows how to respond.

Appendix D

Pleasant and Unpleasant Events as Embodied Signals

This worksheet invites you to notice how your body responds to everyday life.

It is not a practice of balance, positivity, or emotional regulation.
It is a way of staying close to lived experience as it unfolds under unequal conditions.

Some unpleasant events are not personal difficulties but structural realities.
Some pleasant moments are shaped by access, safety, support, or protection that is not evenly available.

The aim is not to fix, reframe, or resolve experience, but to listen.

Time and Pace

You may spend about 10–15 minutes at a time with this practice, if that feels possible.
You may do this once, occasionally, or over several days.
Writing is optional.
Stopping is allowed.

Practice Invitation

Take a few moments to settle.
Recall your day, or a part of it.
You may choose:

- *one unpleasant event*
- *one pleasant event*

You may choose only one, or none at all.
If working with both, you may begin with whichever feels more accessible today.
Pleasant events need not be exciting or joyful. "Okay," neutral, or quietly supportive moments also count.

Aspect	*Unpleasant Event (Optional)*	*Pleasant Event (Optional)*
Event (brief description)		
Body What did you notice in the body? (tightness, warmth, heaviness, release, numbness, movement)		
Emotions What feelings were present, if any? Did they shift or stay steady?		
Sensations Changes in breath, posture, energy, or movement		
Thoughts What stories, meanings, or expectations arose?		
Context (optional) Was this experience shaped by access, power, safety, expectation, or structural conditions (caste, class, gender, disability, queerness, work, family norms)?		

Note: This table is for noticing, not fixing. Your body's responses are information, not instructions.

For Multi-Day Use

Note: You do not need to use this daily. Skipping days is part of the practice.

Date/Moment	*Event (Pleasant or Unpleasant)*	*One Body Signal Noticed*	*One Contextual Factor (if any)*

Index

Pages in *italics* refer to figures, pages in ***bold-italics*** refer to boxes and pages in **bold** refer to tables

For Product Safety Concerns and Information please contact our EU representative GPSR@taylorandfrancis.com Taylor & Francis Verlag GmbH, Kaufingerstraße 24, 80331 München, Germany

Batch number: 10732708

Printed by Printforce, the Netherlands